SNAPSHOTS

A Male Flight Attendant Looks Back

PHILIP BAUER

Ten│16
PRESS

www.ten16press.com - Waukesha, WI

Snapshots: A Male Flight Attendant Looks Back
Copyrighted © 2022 by Philip Bauer
ISBN 9781645384168
First Edition

Snapshots: A Male Flight Attendant Looks Back
by Philip Bauer

Cover Design by: Josh McFarlane
Interior Artwork by: Josh McFarlane

For information, please contact:
shannon@orangehatpublishing.com
414-212-5477

www.ten16press.com
Waukesha, WI

Thank You

My wife, Sarah, has been a willing and tireless companion in this effort—correcting, proofreading and, above all, helping me to keep my tone in check. My sarcasm sometimes leaks out between the lines, but mostly it is less harsh because of Sarah's wise eyes.

My sister, Nancy, a published writer, has given me nonstop encouragement and advice. Without her constant but loving push, these "snapshots" might still be gathering dust in an attic shoebox.

Finally, I would like to thank all of the hundreds, perhaps thousands, of flight attendants whose paths have intersected with mine and who have made me a better person. These are "Menschen" you would want for neighbors.

Table of Contents

Introduction

Imagine. You are older now. One day when you are up in your attic, you see something over in the corner. Nearly concealed by some cobwebs is an old chest. You wonder, after all these years, what could possibly be in it? When you open it, there is a dusty, old shoebox. Inside the shoebox is a scrambled collection of old photographs. Some are black and white, the color has faded from others, and all of them are curled with age. Look, there's old Uncle Ed with his favorite black watch sport coat. Here's one from years ago of your mom and dad, blinking in the light, long before you. And then, as you brush away an imaginary tear, suddenly, there *you* are—sitting on a tricycle, a little out of focus, not knowing anything at all of the stranger you have become. The important pictures, the "good ones"—the weddings, the graduations, the vacations, the Christmas family reunions—are all downstairs in the fine photo albums, gathering the same but a brighter sort of dust. But these photos—the discards, the rejects—are in a dark shoebox, huddled together as if trying to stay warm against the cold trudge of time. You have rescued them, the best ones, and you can't wait to share them with your remaining family. In that spirit, I hope you will open this dusty shoebox and enjoy these old "snapshots."

When I retired from Northwest Airlines in 2008, I had been a flight attendant for twenty-two years. Many flight attendants have careers that dwarf my numerical statistics, which include ballpark figures of 6,000,000 miles, 6,000 takeoffs, an equal number (thank God) of landings, and encounters with about 660,000 passengers. The preponderance of sixes is coincidental. Add to that about 100 nights a year in hotels and somewhere between 12,000 and 16,000 miles (probably more) in hotel vans. Being able to act quickly and decisively in emergencies and having an intimate knowledge of safety emergency equipment required an encyclopedic knowledge which we reviewed and practiced in mock situations every year at Annual Recurrent Training (A.R.T.). I say this in the introduction only because none of that (all of it exasperatingly boring) will be found in these pages (with one exception). Why? Because in my twenty-two years of being a flight attendant, I never opened an aircraft door in an emergency. I never shouted any commands like, "Come this way," or "Go back, exit blocked," or "Sit and slide, help at the bottom." Although trained to do so, I never ripped a fire extinguisher out of its housing to put out an onboard fire. I never attached pads to the chest of a heart attack victim and turned on the defibrillator. I never even used available emergency oxygen on a passenger's behalf. I was never hijacked, and I never was debriefed by the C.I.A. Yet, the training was not in vain. Even though it was never used, we were ready. From a statistical point of view, almost nothing noteworthy happened. Just brief moments and encounters that continue to flicker in my memory—people being people, sometimes at their best and sometimes otherwise. I want to make it clear that the bits and pieces you read here are the outliers. The bulk of my career was characterized by boredom. That is a good thing. Whatever was not boring was populated by the companionship of wonderful people, sprinkled with golden experiences, seasoned with some marvelous layovers and overflowing with a deep and abiding love of flying. Think of it—flying! I expect these tales will have a particular resonance for flight attendants. Perhaps they will spark similar amusing memories of their own. It is my hope that readers will smile a bit from the reflected pleasures that I derived from the writing of this book.

Philip Craig Bauer
Twin Lakes, WI
2022

Clown

One time, I put a red clown ball on my nose for the safety demo and said, "Pay attention, now. This is serious business."

Aisle Seat

All flight attendants will recognize this story, because it is an example of a specific type of passenger. If you are this passenger and recognize yourself, you must change your life. This passenger is an older man. He's wearing his hair pitch-white today. He hasn't got enough of it to protect his scalp from the sun, which gleams pinkish through the wisps. Mismatched shirt and Bermuda shorts, black socks and running shoes complete the picture. He's whining about not getting an aisle seat. I'm able to arrange one for him, but it will require that he move from row sixteen to row seven. He complains about that, because now his bags will be in a bin behind him on arrival. He is not complaining that he will be separated from his wife. I need his boarding card so I can verify with the agent that it will be okay to move him. His wife says, "Don't forget to bring the tickets back, now." I grin and tell her I'm glad she reminded me because I've never done anything so bewildering like this before. A couple of passengers hear my response and smile to themselves. I've won them. As it turns out, row seven is completely open. He has three seats to himself, a whole row. He stretches out, removes his shoes, and it doesn't occur to him to invite his wife to join him. Later on, I point out that things worked out well for him. He has to agree. "Yeah," he says, "God is good." I'm thinking, *"God had nothing to do with it."* I suppose I shouldn't sulk about the fact that he didn't thank me. He didn't thank God either.

Diabetic

A woman gets on this long flight with her husband. They sit together in seats 3A and 3B, first class. She says she's diabetic. This is a late flight from Vegas, and there is no meal service. There is food, though. It's a basket with fruit, snacks, cookies, and chocolate. The agent must have announced in the concourse that there was no meal service on this flight because she's already complaining about it as she is getting on the plane. I offer her something from the in-flight snack basket during the predeparture beverage service. She fuddles through it to see for herself if there will be anything "edible." There isn't, of course. She's diabetic, you know. She waves me off. I don't know why I even bother, but I remember that we have snack boxes for sale in the main cabin. So, after we've reached a "comfortable cruising altitude," I go back to get her one, thinking that there might be something in it for her. I'm the lead flight attendant, so I can write this off to first class. When I offer it to her, she grumbles, "I only have myself to blame. It would never occur to me that there would be a four-hour flight without a meal." Nevertheless, she eats everything in the snack box. (Maybe she ate the box, too). I hope she survives.

At takeoff, her husband had put a hanky over his head. He slept for the whole flight.

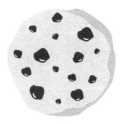

Aisle Seat 2

During the boarding, I'm checking catering. We are serving an ugly snack of some sort in first class. It consists of rice and tough meat in a green, soggy taco shell. It's exactly the kind of meal people choke on because the meat chunks are too big to swallow and too tough to chew. When someone gags and starts to turn blue, I'm wondering how the company will find a way to make it my fault. Rhonda is dealing with a nasty passenger who insists on having an aisle seat. "I don't get on a plane unless I have the aisle!" While Rhonda is busy trying to arrange an aisle seat for her, the woman has taken it upon herself to move people around in the cabin so she can have her precious aisle seat. We're about to push back from the gate and seven or eight people are on their feet, reopening the overhead bins and trying to move their bags around for their convenience upon landing. After Rhonda examines her boarding card in some detail, it becomes apparent that the woman has been reading the wrong one. She had an aisle seat all along. She says, "Oops." Busted! Where are the rude behavior cops when you need them?

Fire Ants

There is a woman getting on the plane. She may be one of the last to board the plane, so I ask her if she is one of the last ones. I'm just trying to establish where we are in the boarding process so I can start preparing the cabin and galley for departure. There's nothing combative or abrasive in my tone, just a simple question. She snarls at me, "What, am I late or something?" I say, "No, I was just trying to see where we were in the boarding." I apologize and tell her sincerely that it wasn't my intention to irritate her in any way. She snaps, "You couldn't irritate me even if you tried." I have a little trouble not laughing out loud. What's that about? A man behind her who has heard the whole encounter looks at me, smiles, and then says to the woman, "Oh, I bet he could!" Later, I say to the man, "I bet it would irritate her if I put some fire ants in her panties." This same woman, after we've been flying for a while, says to me, "If I ever wanted to go on a diet, I'd fly Northwest again." I have no idea what she is talking about. Didn't we give her enough food? Later, I find out she was just being sarcastic about the fat content of the food we did serve. People who know me know that in a sarcasm-off, they want to be on my side. For example, I wanted to tell her the security cameras in the lavatory made her look thin. It was clear from the beginning that it was easy to irritate her. Life irritated her.

(Note: there are no cameras of any sort in the lavatories.)

Big Guys

Two huge men are sitting in 22B and 22C—the aisle seat and the center seat. If we have a light passenger load, we will have to move them forward at takeoff for weight and balance restrictions. To be fair, ordinary sized people would have to be moved too, in similar circumstances. It would have helped if these guys could have hovered at about 20,000 feet, and we could have picked them up enroute, after takeoff. They are pressed against each other so snugly that a side bucket on the beverage cart has to be removed so we can get past them in the aisle. Both of them require double seat belt extenders. which are strained to the limit. There is a wisp of a man sitting in 22A, the window seat. He is flattened up against the wall of the aircraft like cheese spread, effectively blocked in. You know, we make such a big deal about a little bit of luggage on the floor that someone might trip over in an emergency, but these guys bunged the access to the aisle. In an emergency, Mr. Wisp, if he'd been made of water, couldn't have leaked out.

Split Infinitive

There is a group of English teachers onboard. I ask them how they feel about the Oxford dictionary relaxing the rules regarding split infinitives. They laugh. One of them thinks it is a good idea. To once and for all get rid of that old rule is just fine with her

Little Gene

Here's little Gene. He's an unaccompanied minor. The plane has landed and is now parked at the gate. I will take little Gene off the plane after all of the other passengers have deplaned. He gets to sit in first class until that time. During the flight, he is not riding in first class, but from his seat at 22F, he challenges me, "I'll give you seven dollars if I can ride in first." "I'll give you ten dollars." "Twelve dollars." Passengers are offering me even more money to take him up on his offer. Without minimizing how disruptive he is being, I have to admit that he is sort of funny. But, I am not about to move a kid up to first class for the convenience of those in main cabin. Everybody loses on that one. While he's waiting for me to escort him off the plane, he keeps up a patter with the deplaning passengers. "Are you handicapped? Because if you are, you have to sit here and wait for two days." "If you're handicapped, you have to sit here for four days." "Two weeks." Little, adorable Gene.

Dementia

We depart a couple of minutes late, because we have to re-open the aircraft door for a last-minute passenger. It is an elderly woman, and she needs help into the aircraft from her wheelchair. It's a rush. The agent quickly closes the door, and we're left on our own with this completely helpless and confused woman. It becomes clear that she has dementia. She has no notion of seat belts, boarding cards, where to go, or what to do. She seems overly concerned about her bags. "I have seven bags," she explains. "I have twelve bags." "I have four bags." We are trying to depart. A passenger at 5C has to get up so our late arrival can get to her seat at 5A, the window. Annette is on her hands and knees stowing the woman's bag and helping her with her seat belt. She has a business envelope full of money, and she has no sense of its significance. Contained in the glance that Annette and I now exchange is a novel. We don't know who she is, where she is going, or even if anyone is going to meet her in Memphis. When we prepare for arrival, Annette goes up and sits in the 5B seat, because it's worth considering that the woman might do something dangerous or unexpected during the landing. Fortunately, there's a commuting flight attendant, in uniform, who agrees to take the vacant jump seat for landing. Annette and I truly hope that this dear lady makes it safely to where she is going and that caring people will be there for her, but we will never know. It is an aspect of the flight attendant's life to know only the middles of stories.

Take a Breath

I'm working with a flight attendant named Colleen. With Colleen, no thought goes unarticulated. The impulse to fill the silence with the sound of her voice is akin to the impulse of a sky-brick to fall. She can jam a pound of talk into an ounce of idea. "Where are my keys?" "I think I put them in my purse." "Let me look and see." "I don't see them in there." "Did I leave them on the plane?" "Have you seen my keys?" "Where could they be?" "Oh, here they are." If there were some emotional textures or some variations in the quality of her voice-thought mechanisms, she might at least engage, even invite, some response. But alas, her incessant patter is monotonous and never-ending. Periodically, whenever she is turning blue, I have to grab her arm and say, "Colleen! Take a breath." On the final flight of our trip together, we argue about whether or not we will be able to catch the ten o'clock bus to the parking lot. "Yes," I say. We argue about whether the parking lot bus will be late. "No," I say. We argue about whether or not there will be snow on our cars. "No," I say. We argue about whether the tower has cleared us for landing and if the gear is really down. "Yes, and yes." We argue about the final score of the Cubs game. We argue about whether or not the earth is flat, if aliens are living among us, the moon landing. We argue about whether or not my brain has turned to goo. I say, "Yes." She loses every argument.

Puke

Mary and I are trading call lights. The call light at row eleven chimes. Mary says, "Your turn." Why do I get the barfers? The eleventh row is a mess. We have to move several people away from the blast zone. I lose count of how many vomit bags she fills up. Her poor husband is all spotted. People around her are wearing hankies over their faces. I didn't think an adult could have that much loose internal material. You may wonder what a flight attendant does in such situations. Don't wonder. There is no need for you to collect images you can't unsee. You may want to ask how that area gets cleaned. Don't ask. And now when someone says, "I heaved my guts out," I have the receptors to gather in the image.

2-1-1-2

There's a man on the plane who claims to have been thinking about the meaning of the universe for thirty-three years. He has been married for twenty-seven of those years, but his wife won't talk to him anymore. He looks to be a little older than I am, so I hope he's not a harbinger of my future. He has reduced the meaning of the universe to a formula of 2-1-1-2. For example, on this very flight he figures out the relationship between gravity and inertia using his 2-1-1-2 ratios. We are landing, so he doesn't have time to elaborate. He seems to be genuinely excited about his insights. His thinking goes something like this. Let's say you see something, like a tree. There are two things (2)—you thinking and the tree, or maybe your brain and the tree. I'm not too clear. In your mind, however, it becomes one thing (1)—your brain and the tree together. Then there's your brain and you and the tree all together in your mind (1). I'm not making this up. See how everything is symmetrical, like your face?" he concludes (2). "Palindromic," I explain. "So, there's the pre-big-bang and the post-big-bang." He has the pre- and post-big-bang almost figured out using the old 2–1–1–2 pattern. And when he figures it out, "It will change civilization!" God lies between the pre-big-bang and the post-big-bang. That's where God lies." I try to steer him in the direction of Joseph Campbell, but he holds up his hand to stop me from speaking and says, "Right now, I'm *only* reading physics." He has a pen and tablet, and he has been furiously writing down notes for the whole flight. I think I might have heard his brain jingle. He seems to be pleased with me for listening and trying to "get it," and he keeps patting me on the arm and shoulder. Then Mike, the other flight attendant, comes back to the galley, and I have to go away for fear that I' might catch his eye and start to laugh. Who knows, maybe the guy is a conduit to another reality. Well, I guess in fact he is. Two more things need to be mentioned. One is that he tells Mike, "You have to look down the tunnel." And the other is that Mike gets a glance at the man's tablet, and the page he sees is covered with scribbles.

Allergy

A woman comes to the back of the plane in tears because she is allergic to dogs, and there is a dog on the plane. I do what I can for her—get some medicine from the kit and put her in the last row of seats, as far away from the dog as possible. Flight attendant Mitzi isn't particularly sympathetic. She makes comments like, "She'll be all right." Or, "Oh, she's just trying to get some attention." Earlier in the flight, Mitzi made a point about her "philosophy." According to her "philosophy," she doesn't make judgements. She may be right, maybe the woman is looking for attention. If I have a philosophy about passengers, it is that I don't have a philosophy. A style, maybe, or a certain approach, but not a philosophy. If a passenger makes a request, even if it seems unreasonable, I will accommodate that request if I can, unless it compromises safety or the well-being of other passengers. I won't be asking myself, "What would Socrates or Kierkegaard do?" Anyway, the woman with the allergy settles in and doesn't look for any more attention for the rest of the flight. What interests me is the need of some people to claim for themselves virtues, the evidence of which proves otherwise.

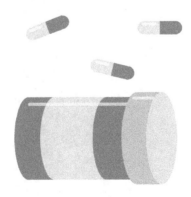

Asshole

The man at 10C is not turning off his cell phone quickly enough for Ken. Ken is a twenty-one-year veteran. I don't see any of the offending behavior, but even before we do our safety demo, Ken is in the galley complaining about the "asshole" in 10C. Later on, I'm serving this man. He's sitting on the aisle across from his wife. He wants to know the name of my colleague, because he's an "asshole." What a coincidence, two assholes on one flight. I tell him that his name is Ken. I don't know Ken's last name. I tell Ken that 10C wanted to know his name. Ken now wants to know from 10C why he asked *me* for his name when it was to *him* that he wanted to talk. Later, for a second time, I'm told that Ken is an "asshole." And Ken reminds me that 10C is an "asshole." Score tied, 2–2. Well, by God, this isn't going to end here. We're taking this to the Supreme Court. We might even request the death penalty. And I don't even know what it's all about. Now I'm in the aisle doing Ken's work because he's in the galley writing up this enormous report. I'm not going to be very happy when the company calls and wants to schedule a Q&A on my time. Not one passenger comes to Ken's defense. Color me shaking my head in disbelief. Twenty-one years!

Beaver Water

"Is that water filtered?" This is the question posed to me by a sweet old lady on her way to Venezuela. I say, "Well, I don't know. Let's take a look at the label." While I'm examining the label, she says, "'Cause there's beavers in the water, you know, and they leave their droppings." I understand that this is a "have to be there moment," but still, *beaver droppings?* I say just loud enough for some others to hear me, "I'm pretty sure there aren't any beaver droppings in this water." As my life as a flight attendant continues, whenever a passenger asks me what the beverage selections are, I always add, "Venezuelan Beaver Water" to my list. And when they ask me what Venezuelan Beaver Water is, I have the pleasure of retelling the story.

Beginner

During a beverage service in the main cabin, a passenger asks me for a sparkling water and a red wine. There's a moment of insignificant confusion because I don't hear the part about the red wine. But there's this old guy sitting across the aisle, and he says to me, "Oh, you must be a new hire, huh?" In my mind, I roll my eyes, sigh, and think, "Be careful, old man, I haven't served you yet." I've been flying for seventeen years, and what I want to say is, "Well, I'm a lot newer than you and always will be." A little background. Originally, this flight was scheduled to be a beverage-only service both in first class and the main cabin. But when there are timetable changes, there are often service changes as well. This flight now has a full meal service in first class. Main cabin stays the same. Earlier, this man who has chided me had an opportunity to upgrade to first class, but he passed on his chance because he thought there would be no meal. His wife, however, did take her upgrade—husband and wife, she in first class, he in the main cabin. Back when we were boarding the plane, there was a woman in first class whom I was especially nice to, helping her with her luggage and getting her something to drink. I was unaware of any connection between her and the old man in the back. Later in the flight, however, the woman comes back to see how the old boy is doing. I happen to be standing in the aisle near him when she (his wife) puts her hands on my shoulders, motherlike, and tells her husband what a good flight attendant I am and how attentive I was to her needs. I say, "Yeah, and I'm just a beginner."

Bob the Good Flight Attendant

Bob is a good flight attendant, and he spends a considerable amount of time telling you how good he is. He tells you how nice he is to passengers and how disappointed he is in Northwest for not acting on his suggestions, and yet the company treats him like *he* is the one with a problem. Bob is the lead flight attendant, but right now he's sitting on the jump seat in the back of the plane, far away from his first-class passengers, telling Mary what a good flight attendant he is and how he wants to change things so that everything will be better. I'm not interested in Bob or his experiences or his philosophy. I wander up to first class and take care of three or four of his passengers who have requests. Refill a drink, answer a question, a little small talk. I stroll back to the aft galley, and Bob is still chatting with Mary. They are sitting on the jump seat facing aft. They cannot see forward into the cabin. I'm standing against the galley counter, and I see a man way up in the front of the plane get up and wend his way through the aisle toward me. He asks me for some orange juice. At this moment, I don't realize he is from first class. He says he was sleeping, so he missed the service. I ask him if he wants some pretzels. Bob turns from where he is sitting with Mary and says to me, "I already gave him some pretzels."

There is a lot to unpack here. Still, I will try. 1) Bob has positioned himself as far away from his first-class passengers as possible and in such a way that he cannot even see them. 2) He speaks to *me* and not directly to the passenger (who is standing right there) as if I am some sort of information conduit. And 3) He ignores performing a reasonable kindness. Jesus, Bob, give him another bag of pretzels! Bob has done everything he possibly can to separate himself from his job, his first-class passengers! But Bob is a good flight attendant. He'll tell you so. It is clear that Bob's calling is in management.

Pregnant Woman

A pregnant woman is eating her lunch. Her tray table rests slightly askew on her bulge. As I walk past in the aisle, she bumps her plastic bottle of water, and it falls to the floor and rolls under her seat. I can easily retrieve it, and as I hand it back to her, I say, "I'm glad your water didn't break."

Heavy

A frail woman gets on the plane and asks me if I would be willing to help her with her roller bag. I am always willing to help. Some flight attendants are more likely to say, "You pack it, you rack it." Some. I am not one of those. When I go to help her, I realize quickly that it is the heaviest piece of luggage I have ever lifted. In jest, I say to the woman, "Have you considered just renting your bowling balls when you arrive?" She responds, "Do you want to know what's in there?" I say, "Sure." "It is the urn with the ashes of my dead husband." I am, of course, chagrined. But she seems amused by my comment, smiles, and thanks me for my assistance. I don't know who helped her get the bag down from the overhead, but if I see her anywhere near a bowling alley in Cleveland, I'll kick her in the ashes.

Indiana Time

To be fair to the passenger who lodged a complaint against me, I am not familiar with the idiosyncrasies of the Indiana time structures. So, when I announce the time during the arrival speech, I am wrong. A deplaning passenger with snoot to spare, oozing with condescension, says to me, "If you don't know anything about time zones, you shouldn't say anything at all." Now if you were this passenger, is this something you would say to a flight attendant who had clearly made a mistake? I hope for the sake of Mr. Snoot that he doesn't arrive an hour late for his brain transplant, since everybody knows there are no clocks in the Indianapolis airport.

Fire

If you are flying into a large airport, such as O'Hare or Minneapolis, and see great billows of black smoke rising into the sky from a spot near the airport, it is probably a fire drill exercise being conducted by the firefighters at the airport. It is one way to dispose of worn aircraft tires, and it provides experience to those who would fight other fires. Nevertheless, to see this as you are preparing to land can be unsettling.

Fingers

I'm in the aisle picking up the trash after the meal service. Something resembling a human being snaps at me, "If you take anything off that tray, I'll break your fingers." The language mechanisms of my brain are unable to process the significance of his words. I can't even understand his comment as a joke. It's becoming clear now: I'm one of a bunch of hairy creatures sitting around a waning fire at night. The females are huddled behind us in the caves. We are all gnawing on the bones of a tapir we've managed to kill. I reach for a bone near the ape next to me, and he grunts, "Touch that bone and I'll break your fingers."

Breezy

The lead, Carole, seems pleasant enough. She takes the lead position even though she isn't junior. That tells me she probably likes it, and I get the feeling she does it well. In fact, her announcements whiz along so breezily that by the time she's finished reading them, the sound hasn't reached the back of the airplane.

Budapest

There is a man on the plane wearing all green—green blazer, green slacks, and a green baseball cap that says "Budapest" on it. He's sitting next to one of our unaccompanied minors. We are in our descent when he comes to the back galley and tries to get me to give the unaccompanied minor something to eat. Maybe one of our three-dollar snack boxes. His demand suggests that I'd have to be a beast if I didn't give the kid something. The kid, by the way, is shaking his head. He doesn't want anything. I'm not fond of being whipsawed in this way. If I don't give the kid a complimentary snack box, I'm a jerk. But if I do, Budapest is the hero. I suggest to Mr. Budapest that if he wants the kid to have something to eat, he can buy a snack box for him. He shrugs that off and uses the opportunity to complain about Northwest. He's flown with Lufthansa and Delta, and you don't even get peanuts anymore with Northwest. "With your company, you don't get shit." I tell him that isn't true. "I can get you some shit," I say. And by so saying, I just did.

All On One Flight

The man at 27C stands and complains that we don't have any food. "This is bullshit," he announces. If I had known that he wanted to give a speech, I could have offered him the aircraft megaphone. I reply, "So is the food, when we have it." I figure I'll get scolded for that response, but I couldn't resist. It is not my style to be sarcastic to paying customers, but I just couldn't help myself. Any person, I figure, who is so self-absorbed that he can stand up and use the word "bullshit," in reference to the company I work for, with such exaggerated conviction, is unlikely to be aware of the social lubrications that allow masses of people to slide together closely without altercation. In a word, courtesy. And therefore, justifying myself, I assume he wouldn't understand the subtleties of metaphor or sarcasm. Enough passengers enjoy my rejoinder to stroke my ego.

Then a passenger yells at me because another passenger has his doggies out of their cage. I don't get why I'm the one being yelled at, or why I'm being yelled at for anything at all. Yell at the doggie guy. I approach the dog's owner, who (by the way) is, in fact, in violation. He sasses me, "Don't worry about it." *Don't worry about it?* I ask him if he thinks I look worried and then tell him that he needs to put his dogs in their cage now. I wonder if that response would work if he got stopped for speeding. "You were going ninety miles an hour, sir, in this forty-five zone." "Don't worry about it," Yeah, that'll work.

And then there's a woman who is crabby about her blanket and pillow. I never found out why. One can only imagine. The avenues of her crabbiness may stretch out toward the stars. To speculate about why she is so angry could conceivably lead into another dimension. I feel some grief, but this is a flight to anywhere, nowhere. Fixing her is not something for a flight attendant. She gets off the plane without a word. She has no idea that there are sincere flight attendants, who, although we could do nothing, wish her well and yearn for her well-being.

Another rude creature says to me about her bag, "Do something with this?" This is not a good thing to say to a flight attendant, especially to a flight attendant who already has an armful of passenger carry-ons. There are too many good, ripe replies. The trouble is, she makes no eye contact, or waits for any acknowledgement. She just lets go of her bag in my general direction. The strap catches my little finger, and the weight of her bag bends it sharply toward the back of my hand. My pinkie explodes in pain and in an instant becomes a loose, floppy thing. I lose control of the bags I'm holding, which fall into the lap of the passenger at the aisle, who says perceptively, "I don't think your finger is supposed to bend that way." I spend a couple of moments agonizingly resetting my pinkie in its socket. The woman, even though she is aware of my distress, is nevertheless unconcerned, unapologetic, and uncommunicative. She just sits there, all snuggled into herself like a turtle, fuming, a reptile wearing human skin.

Near the end of the flight, a guy comes out of the aft lavatory with his pants down and his zipper open. "I just need to tuck my shirt in," he explains.

All of this on one flight. Surreal.

Steamer

My flight attendant colleagues on this trip are Dede and Bob. Dede is the epitome of the scatterbrained blonde. Her conversation is animated, overheated, and dramatic. She wants to make a point with every other sentence. To punctuate her points, she grabs my arm. She can hardly say "steamer," to me without painfully grabbing and squeezing my arm. I've learned to greet her by saying, "Don't touch me!" My wife is beginning to wonder about the black and blue marks I'm coming home with. One time, I mentioned to Dede that a dog had left a steamer in the snow in our yard. The word "steamer" for some reason dissolved her into spasms of uncontrollable laughter. Whenever I see her now, the word "steamer" has replaced other, more standard greetings. Me: "Hi Dede, don't touch me." She: "Steamer."

We are now on our way to San Diego, and Dede is relentlessly trying to get me to go to Tijuana with her. I am just as firmly refusing. Bob is a former marine. He's not as tall as I am, but he is built solid and stocky and has a bullet-shaped head resting on a neck so thick he can see it with his own eyes. He's from New York, and he's trying to encourage me to go with Dede to Tijuana.

"Yeah, you should go to tee-a-wanna with 'er. Ya kin git anyting you wanna git in tee-a-wanna. Ya know, five, ten bucks, maybe a quickie. Werx fer me!"

"Denn YOU go ta tee-a-wanna with 'er," I say. Daz werx fer ME!

Cart Designer

How a flight attendant sets up his or her cart for the service is a very personal thing. I prepare my cart in such a way, as do all flight attendants, to minimize effort. I may arrange the items on my cart slightly differently depending on time of day, my position in the aisle, ease of access to the galley, etc. I've been doing this now for about twenty years, and my service is as smoothly greased as I can get it. I'm in the aisle, and a lady says to me, "Why don't you set up your cart like the other flight attendant? Then you wouldn't have to reach over so far for your ice, and it would be more convenient." It's a reasonable question, and I explain why. "Have it your way, then," she sniffs, folds her arms over her chest, looks away from me, and refuses a drink. I will have it my way, thank you very much.

On this same flight is a former Northwest flight attendant with her mother and her two children, one of them still an infant. The mother is a meddling piece of work. She is on her feet for most of this two-hour flight. When I pull my cart to the front to start my service, she actually reaches into my ice bucket with her bare hand, helps herself to a couple of ice cubes, and pops them into her mouth. I have to empty the bucket and replenish with a fresh load. The flight is constantly about her. She would be the type to rearrange my beverage cart for my convenience.

Catering

I'm in Raleigh-Durham, my hand wrapped around a nice, chilly traditional lager beer. A pizza is on the way. Seen from that myopic point of view, life is good. However, the flight from Mecca (Minneapolis) was a calamity. If the caterers had maliciously planned to sabotage the service, their efforts could not have been more successful. At least three meals were completely destroyed and could not have been served. Well, I suppose they *could* have been served, if dignity and hygiene weren't issues. The dessert cakes had been turned over, completely off their plates and smashed onto the nearby fruit plates. Together, the flattened cakes and fruit looked like urine-soaked guano. The cake-fruit hybrid was then smeared across the bottoms of the above trays, squirting out in oozy colors, forming splotches like Jackson Pollack art. I say "at least three meals" because other meals were jammed up and smashed as well, but I was able, in the galley, to consolidate, clean up, and combine some of the other meals to make them suitable for consumption. If there hadn't been three refusals, there would have been first-class passengers who could not have been served. Words that rattle around in the brains of flight attendants like "professional," "cleanliness," "smile," and "glamour" seemed suddenly to have lost their connectivity. I had to reprocess to gather in their meaning, which newly seemed to have nothing to do with my job. If only that were all!

The mix kit. This is a metal box with metal shelves. On the shelves are drawers containing sodas and mixes. But one of the drawers inside the mix kit does not fit the shelf, and it is jammed in so tightly and awkwardly that it will not budge. The other flight attendants tried to dislodge it. A bruising first-class passenger tried to dislodge it. In fact, I took the whole kit out of its bustle, removed the two drawers that weren't jammed, and tried with my foot to dislodge the drawer, but to no avail. Dynamite may not have budged it. Consider that image, by the way, from a first-class passenger's point of view. So, I had to go back through the main cabin to the aft galley several times in the middle of my first-class service for beverages I should have been able to get from the jammed drawer. I'd hate to see it in a landfill, so I thought maybe they could melt it down for first-class spoons. A guy in the last first-class row said, "You sure have a good personality for this job." Maybe he'd been watching and had an idea of what I'd been through. I said, "Yeah, I got an Oscar for acting. Just think, lucky you declined to eat, because you wouldn't have gotten a meal anyway."

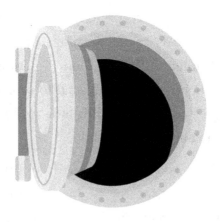

Hotel Pens

Now I'll tell you about the cheap hotel pens. On this trip, inexplicably, I brought only one with me. I usually carry two or more, because passengers often ask to borrow a pen, and I always just give them one. Well, on the very first leg, someone asks if they can borrow a pen and I give them my one and only cheap hotel pen. I know that I have a couple of my own pens I can use if need be. And, of course, I will be picking up more cheap hotel pens as the trip progresses. Well, the two of my own pens actually run out of ink on the first day and I have to borrow a pen from Michelle. This represents the first time ever that I've had to borrow a pen. Then, I manage to replace a pen from the Baymont in Detroit. Then for the next two nights, which I spend at a Radisson in Tampa and the Merrimack in Manchester, there are *no* free pens in the room. But, here at the Ramada, finally, there two complimentary pens. Whew. Now I'm back in business, just in time for the end of the trip.

Cherry

I know a flight attendant named Cherry. If she married Brad Pitt, or Chuck Berry . . . You could make a game of this. What if Tuesday Weld married Billy Sunday, got a divorce, and then married Joe Friday?

Potty Break

Cindi, Sandi, and I are between flights in the Minneapolis airport. We haven't gotten to know each other yet. It's early in the trip, and they defer the lead position to me. Cindi, who's wearing the dress version of her uniform, needs to go to the restroom. Sandi and I sit down, watch her bags, and wait for her to come out. She returns so quickly I can hardly believe it. It's not in my experience for any woman to go to the restroom and return so quickly. She says, "If you wear the slacks, it takes so long. You gotta unbuckle, slide the pants down, do your business, slide the pants up, tuck in, rebuckle. But if you wear the dress, you just slip it up, sit down, and it's all over." I stop dead in my tracks, and when they turn to look at me, I have both of my fists pressed to my forehead. "Wait a minute, wait a minute, I'm getting an image." That line has its hoped-for effect, but I really owe it to Steve Bertrand of WGN radio, Chicago.

Cowboy

We had another fun one today coming from Tampa. A guy got on the plane wearing a cowboy hat and shouting things like, "Yee-haw!" He was plastered and never should have been able to get on the plane. He wasn't rude and obnoxious—just obnoxious. The first thing he asked me was how long it would be before he could get a beer. Then he got stuck in the lavatory. I thought he was going to rip the door off, but then he figured how to get out. During the service, I refused him liquor. He asked for a beer. I said, "I don't think so." He said, "No beer?" I said, "Nope, not now." "Any liquor at all?" "'Fraid not." The people in the row behind him thanked me for not serving him.

Nuts

A woman gets on the plane with her son, who, she explains, is allergic to nuts. I am helping in first class during the boarding process. She wants to know if nuts are a part of our service. I tell her that Northwest Airlines no longer caters peanuts, but we serve almonds in first class. She says that her son is allergic to all nuts. Our policy is that we do not restrict the almond service, and if she is uncomfortable with that ruling, the agents will help her make other arrangements. I show her the page from our manual, clearly stating the policy. She is determined to stay on the plane, anyway. I might point out here that this is not a flight attendant issue. This should have been resolved before she boarded. The captain is of no help and the lead has no clue what to do. So, I ask the woman, "Suppose we serve the almonds in first class and your son has an episode?" She says, "You will just have to land the plane." I assume she's using "you" in the second-person plural sense.

I interrupt the narrative here to say how sorry I am that she has this burden to bear. It isn't anything she deserves. It must be heartbreaking for a parent to have a child with harsh roadblocks to a full life. Yet, many of us, if not all, have some burden—burdens that we don't deserve, but we have them and they are ours. One can always ask for help, but one may not demand help. Others are not to blame, nor are they responsible for our burdens.

This woman, however, has gone a step too far. She is essentially sanctioning the unsolicited approval of 150 other people and the crew to share responsibility for her burden. I don't believe she has the right to speak on behalf of dozens of strangers. All those people are going to Phoenix, too. They have obligations, appointments and deadlines, and yes, burdens of their own. They are not going to like landing in Oklahoma City because your boy has allergies.

So, what do I do? It seems obvious that I have to cave to the woman. I have to defy the company policy and not serve the almonds in first class. After the aircraft door is closed, I announce that we have a passenger on board with a nut allergy, and would all passengers please be so kind as to refrain from eating any nuts they might have brought on the plane. My reasoning: I imagine a worst-case future where an Oklahoma City newspaper runs the headline "Northwest Airlines Emergency Landing Due to Flight Attendant Negligence."

I might point out that this whole situation is thankless. I am not forward for the deplaning, but it is a long flight. We don't have to make a special landing, and the woman's little boy doesn't go into anaphylactic shock. There is plenty of time to convey a bit of appreciation for collectively sharing her burden.

Peanut Races

Speaking of peanuts, there is a jump seat at the very back of the 727 built for two. Kathy and I are sitting on it facing forward. It is not a bicycle. It is not romantic. We are just moments away from landing, and on the floor in front of us we have lined up a row of peanuts. It will delight us to see how far forward the peanuts will bounce and roll when the pilots bring the plane to its roaring stop. The winners of this race often make it all the way up to the cockpit door. I know, it sounds stupid, but it would delight you, too. Good thing there aren't any passengers with peanut allergies. It would be like crop-dusting.

Cuckoo Cornball

We are boarding a flight to Kansas City. We haven't been catered yet, so all of the service carts from the previous flight are still onboard. They will be removed when the carts for our flight are catered. Tom is asking about the predeparture service, and I tell him we cannot open the liquor cart because they are security-sealed for removal. A passenger in first class goes a little cuckoo and shouts at me, "What? You can't open the liquor cart?" I explain to him that we will get him something to drink as soon as the liquor cart for this flight arrives. I also report to him that his eyes are the size of golf balls. He isn't amused. "But will I get something before takeoff?" That's the plan. We are, in fact, catered in time, and everybody gets a drink. But I'm thinking, "Oh boy, this cornball is going to be a handful," and I'm preparing myself for quick responses and funny comebacks. He sleeps all the way to Kansas City. In flight, I don't serve him a single drink.

Line Check

We have pushed back from the gate. We taxi to a spot on the tarmac and park. We have not moved for a few minutes when a passenger orders me to go to the cockpit and find out what's going on. I go to the cockpit, and the captain says that mechanics are conducting a "line check." I say, "What is a line check?" He tells me that all American aircraft must undergo periodic equipment safety checks. They are specific, they don't take long, and they are determined by the length of time or number of flights between checks. That is what he tells me. I return to the man and tell him that a line check is being conducted on our airplane, specifically for our navigation lights. At this point, the man stands up, waves his arm about as if he's a politician at a fundraiser and to all, or anyone, who can hear him bellows, "Did you hear that, folks? Line check! They will tell us anything!" It is still early in my career as a flight attendant, and I have no emotional reserves or experience to deal with such abrupt rancor. It's a good thing, because whatever the force is that's fueling his wrath, it blows right through me. Ordinarily, this might have hobbled or disoriented me. Later in my years, it would occur to me just to laugh. In this case, there is nothing. I look at him and speak just as calmly as if I were saying, "Do you want fries with that?" I say, "You are embarrassing me, and you are probably embarrassing yourself. I did what you asked me to do, and I reported to you what the pilot told me. Now, if you look out the window on your left, you will see a mechanic on a ladder replacing the red light on the end of the wing." At this point, a dozen or more heads turned to look. "And if you look to the right, you will see another mechanic doing the green one on the right wing. If it's all the same to you, I prefer to have navigation lights in working order before we take off."

All in all, it is a good experience, because going forward I have a touchstone to remind me how to handle a loud, obnoxious passenger.

Saint

There is a young woman onboard who is tending to her needy parents. The mother has had a stroke and needs a straight-backed chair for getting up and down the aisle. I saw the father in the concourse before we got on the plane. The front of his pants was all wet. The daughter must be leaning toward sainthood, taking care of an incontinent father and a mother whose arms and legs are all twisted from the results of the stroke. Later in the flight, the father goes to the lavatory, and when he comes out, the whole back of his pants is wet, sopping actually. I suggest to the daughter that we put a blanket down underneath him. Fine. The area around him is now as ripe as freshly "spread" Wisconsin farmland. I have a longing sympathy for the daughter. The smell of whatever the old fella brought back to his seat with him from the lav is disturbingly evident to all who sit in the last several rows. People are trying to be kind, but many are breathing through their hankies. Maybe I can find some air freshener in the pocket behind the last row of seats. Not. For them, Orange County is still three to four hours away. The other flight attendant is sitting on her jump seat with a coffee bag on her face. "I can't stand this," she says. How this family trio—a reverse Nativity scene—manages, I will never know. Our crew is replaced in Minneapolis, but this family continues on their way to Orange County. Godspeed, dear creatures of the universe.

Lawyer

A guy gets off the plane in Minneapolis and complains that it was the worst flight he's ever been on. He claims that his life and the life of the passengers was endangered because some people were using cell phones. And, by the way, he's a lawyer and he's going to sue Northwest Airlines. According to James, the other flight attendant, this "lawyer" had to be admonished to turn off his own cell phone. Twice! If this man thinks this was the worst flight he's ever been on, we are thinking he must not be a frequent flyer. And if he were really a lawyer, he might have saved his comments for letterhead correspondence to Northwest Airlines and not voiced his intentions so vocally for all those around him to hear. This is a fact: When you have two flight attendants and 108 passengers, the ratio of them to us is in the "them" favor. When passengers think that the flight attendant has diverted attention, they feel free to do just about anything they want. When the flight attendant is in the aisle in the middle of a service, who knows what goes on. Couples can sneak into the lav. People can get up and wander around even if the seat belt sign is on. They can take their pet out of the cage and hold it (against rules) barking or meowing on their lap. They can be in our galley, they can take stuff from our carts, they can help themselves to coffee or soda. And, of course, they can try to use their cell phones. I'm sure that sort of thing happens all the time. And why our "lawyer" didn't report to us that someone was using a cell phone is beyond explanation. If he truly thought his life was being endangered . . . well, maybe his life wasn't being so much endangered after all, and the odds were more in favor of a legal action. In fact, had he been aware of a dangerous situation and *not* pointed it out to the flight attendants, I would think *he* should be the one sued.

When I think of all the "hats" that flight attendants wear—in addition to that of waiter, waitress, safety officer, security agent, as well as babysitter, bartender, lavatory custodian, cleaner, waste management rep, teacher, caregiver, and in emergencies, lifesaver ... we're the complaint department, the information desk and, last but not least, we are agents of the federal government with authority to enforce all F.A.R.s (Federal Aviation Regulations) that apply to in-flight rules and safety. I just hope we don't have to add one more job to the list: defendant.

Flatware

Security measures were abruptly heightened after 9/11, sometimes to extreme levels. Shortly after the new security procedures were in place, pilots were allowed to carry a gun onto the plane. The following is a regular occurrence: One of the two pilots has a gun. They approach the metal detectors. The one with the gun goes to a designated lane, while the other stays in line and takes off his or her shoes like everybody else, like any other passenger, like us flight attendants. I could never figure this out. One pilot with a gun, the other taking his shoes off. When I see this, I rub my eyes, because I think they have betrayed me and are sending stupid signals to my brain. It is my belief that crew members do not need a full security screening. Why? Because we have already been drug tested, checked with a Breathalyzer, urine sampled, background-checked, bonded and fingerprinted. Fingerprinted! We carry two forms of photo ID. They have our DNA. And, after we pass through security, we *are* the security. Maybe the agents get warm fuzzies from showing off to the flying public just how thorough they are. "Wow, look at that. Even a pilot is taking off his shoes." All of this, of course, doesn't stop a TSA agent from confiscating my flatware. I chose to carry this particular stainless-steel set because it is identical to the flatware we use for passengers in first class. I guess he doesn't see the irony or the madness in removing from my possession items that are perfectly acceptable, normal, and even necessary on the plane. I try to explain, "So, passengers are entitled to items forbidden to the crew? That makes no sense." He says, "Why don't you just leave your flatware on the plane? That way, it will always be there for you." "Do you think I'm on the very same plane for three, four, or five days in a row? Do you think the plane is my office I go every day like some business owner?" I'm amused by his inability to see his error. But he's getting tired of me, so he shouts, "It's not amusing!" Actually, he's right. It's moronic. To be fair, most security agents are polite and friendly. It's just too bad that this authoritarian agent is in Milwaukee, the airport I have to go through every time I commute to work. I've had one other unfortunate episode with TSA in Los Angeles. But it is just too hard to describe. And when I think of it, my blood pressure erupts.

Sally

Sally Struthers was on our flight one day. She was very nice.

Dog Food

Here's a passenger complaining that we were giving them food that isn't fit for dogs. It escalates into us supposedly treating the passengers like dogs. Oh please! I have to step up and point out 1) About eighty other people are eating the food and haven't started barking... yet. 2) Nobody is treating anybody like dogs. We are treating them like cattle. Didn't he get the memo? He had his hopes set on a little something from first class. Right. I find him a "special" vegetarian meal that hasn't been claimed that looks more like dog food to me (a gray mushy substance that contains what looks like a bean or two, disguised) than the original snack sandwich. A "special meal," by the way, is one ordered by the passenger prior to the flight. It may be vegan, kosher, salt-free, etc. Anyway, the man seems to be happy with it. He is special.

Steak

The only thing a passenger said to me today was, "And don't burn my steak, neither!" That was all. No hello, no greeting, no goodbye.

Kosher

We are early in the boarding process. First class is pretty much settled in, and the man at 1C asks me if his "special" kosher meal has been catered. I will check for him, and of course, his suspicions are confirmed. No, it has not been catered. We are still fifteen to twenty minutes from departure, so I go to the captain and ask him if he can get catering to bring a kosher meal to our flight. He agrees to try. The minutes tick by, and when the agent comes to close the door, there is no kosher meal. I go to the man and apologize. I say to him, "I'm sorry your kosher meal did not get here, but, if I could chop off my left arm and have it magically transform into your meal, I would do that . . . No! Wait, I wouldn't do that! But, I am sorry, we tried." He didn't hear much of what I said after, "No! Wait," because he was laughing so hard.

Dove Bar

Much of my flying was on a state-of-the-art Boeing 747–400. Still, even this plane had no refrigeration. We kept food cold, including the Dove Bars, with dry ice. The Dove Bars were considered part of the business class dessert menu, but our instruction was that they were to be available throughout the flight. It could be two to three hours into the flight before we even got to the dessert, so we had to ensure that the Doves would not melt before then. And so, by a certain necessity, the Dove Bars are still pretty hard when we serve them. This does not meet the approval of a passenger who insists that they should be served ready to eat. I have never taken it upon myself to be superior to anyone in any line of work I am not familiar with. I would not try to educate my dentist, or to give lectures to my plumber. But anybody can be superior to a flight attendant. We are just flight attendants. And, from a certain sensible and reasonable point of view, this passenger is correct. Things shouldn't be served ill or unprepared. But I remind him that we are on a thirteen-hour flight, in a metal tube that is streaking through the air at 39,000 feet—4,000 miles away from our destination—and that we don't have refrigerators and must use dry ice to keep things cold.

His response to that is, essentially, "So what? You should remove them from the dry ice at such a time prior to the dessert service that they will then be ready to eat."

And I say, "We would love to do that, but we have no notion of how many passengers will be ready to eat their Dove Bar. We have sixty people in business class, and some will be sleeping."

He says, "You should have a notion of approximately what percentage of people will be sleeping and start to thaw an amount according to the need demonstrated by past experience."

And I say, "That will not account for the passengers who will wake up at different times and will want their Dove Bar. Our instructions are to make them available at any time during the flight."

His answer is, "So you want me to sit with a frozen Dove Bar on my tray table in business class and wait for it to thaw?"

Of course, the answer is well, yeah. But I don't say that. This is what I think of saying: "Right, I get it now. It's all about you, isn't it? It's not about all of the other passengers who may request their Dove

Bar at different times. What we are doing for you and any other passenger is to keep the Dove Bars on dry ice so they will be available whenever. After we serve one, you can take charge of the eating. That may include a few moments for it to thaw. That seems inevitable. By your logic, perhaps I should suggest to management that we take reservations for the use of the lavatories. That way, any passenger could take a dump at exactly the precise moment it had been scheduled. No waiting in line. No need to regard the excretory requirements of any other passengers. No clumsy flight attendants dictating the demands of your bowels. Freedom. It goes without saying that a passenger could still, at any time, dump on a flight attendant."

Going on, I don't like it when what seems to be a conversation turns into an argument. Instead, I say the thing that stops the whole encounter. "You know, you are right." He seems satisfied, turns, and walks away, probably thinking he has just scored another victory against some inferior life-form. If I suggest anything to management, it will be to serve brownies or cake for dessert. Maybe one of those luscious French pastries.

Earthquake

June 30, 2004.

A woman comes out of the lav. She's maybe forty years old. Blonde, friendly, nice-looking. She wants to talk.

She: "So, how long have you been doing this?"

Me: "I just finished my seventeenth year."

S: "I used to work for the airlines, America West, but on the ground, never in the air. Just for the benefits."

M: "Nice."

S: "Do you think the terrorists are going to strike before the election?"

M: "That's pretty hard to know."

S: "If they do strike, how do you think it will be?"

M: "Ya got me."

S: "Do you think Bush will win?"

M: "It looks like a pretty close race."

S: "You know, I think flight attendants should carry some protection. Like, who would think a blonde like me would be carrying a weapon?"

M: "I don't know, I could imagine a woman like you would carry some protection." (She doesn't hear my mind wander.)

S: "Hey, have you heard about the earthquake?"

M: "You mean the one in Illinois last week?"

S: "No, no, the one in California. It's been predicted by a lot of scientists and some guy in Norway."

M: "Oh? Norway?"

S: "There's a nine-month period between January and September 5, 2004, when it will happen. Not *if* but *when*."

M: "It's June now."

S: "It will be along a fault line in California that includes Palm Springs and Las Vegas. It will happen because of all the sinners."

M: "What?"

S: "The sinners!"

M: "Can sinners do—"

S: "I went to a town meeting in Palm Springs and learned how to survive an earthquake."

M: "Will the sinners survive an earth—"

S: "Never, never, never turn off your gas, because when the gas comes back on again, the poor gas people will have to go around turning everybody's gas back on."

M: "I didn't know that."

S: "And you should save your plastic bags from the grocery store. When you go to the bathroom, put the bag in the toilet, poop in the bag, and bury the bag in your backyard."

M: "I poop a lot."

S: "So when the earthquake happens, you'll remember me, the girl who said it would."

M: "Ok."

(The earthquake did not happen, but for some reason I remembered the girl anyway.)

Humorist

A guy gets on the plane, and one of the first things he says to me is, "Where did they get you? From the 'hire the handicapped' listings?" I get it, this guy is a humorist, and since a flight attendant might be the lowest of the low, he can be a brute and get away with it. I don't give him the satisfaction of even rolling my eyes. I just say, "Yeah, they used the same list for the pilots." But, he doesn't get it, and it doesn't end there. He carries a little book that must be filled with insults, because every time I pass him in the aisle, he has located in his files some new unfunny jab. "Did your mother dress you today?" and one-liners of that ilk. I can almost hear the groans of nearby passengers. Finally, I cannot take his stupid, unkind remarks any longer, and I say, "50,000 manholes in New York, and you had to drop in here?" This riles him. He stands up and challenges me, "Is that supposed to be funny? You call that humor?" I say, with a completely straight face, "That was main cabin humor. The jokes are better up in first class." For the rest of the flight, I do not hear another peep.

Announcements

The plane has landed and is taxiing toward the gate. The lead flight attendant is making his arrival address. He has done this a million times, so he has it memorized. Sort of. It is meant to be read word-for-word as it appears in the little Northwest mini-manual. If he ad-libs, it might sound something like this:

"Northwest Airlines would like to be the first to welcome you to Bismarck. Please remain seated until the captain has turned off the seat belt sign. This will be your one and only indication that is safe to release your seatbelt and move about the cabin. Use caution when opening the overhead bins, as items may have shifted during takeoff and landing. A uniformed customer service agent will be available at the top of the jetway to answer any questions you may have regarding connecting flights, baggage claim, restrooms, and other airport facilities. We apologize for crash-landing in that cornfield back there near Fargo and hope this has not inconvenienced you too greatly. We are grateful that we did not have to resort to eating human flesh, as sometimes happens in mountain crashes. Once again, thank you for choosing Northwest Airlines. We appreciate your business. Have a nice day."

My comments on the above announcement follow. Actually, this example is still not as bad as some of the interminable massacres of language that have blistered my brain. Passengers must be thinking that either the flight attendant is naturally prolix (maybe the son of an auctioneer), or the Northwest announcement writers are unable to think clearly. It is hard for me to imagine that

everybody on this flight is coming to Bismarck for the first time. Also, there are many, not "one and only," indications that it is safe to get up (the engines shut down, you see baggage carts moving toward the plane, etc.). And "move about the cabin"? You mean, like, get up and get off? The aisle isn't a ballroom. You won't have free-wheeling motion options. And, when the first bag slips out of the bin and conks a noggin, the passengers will suddenly get caution-religion. I never saw anything like that happen. Also, everybody knows from whom one might get answers to questions. Telling people where to go to ask questions would make me feel like a parent. And, of course, we didn't crash, so that was just silly stuff. You see, nobody was listening, anyway.

I have been a lead flight attendant on occasion, and I much prefer this:

"Welcome to Bismarck. Please stay seated until the plane is parked at the gate. Thank you for choosing Northwest Airlines. We appreciate your business. Have a nice day."

Blankets and Empty Bins

I'm at the back of the aircraft. We are just starting the boarding process. Every bin is empty, except for one small bin at the back of the plane where we have folded neatly and stowed the blankets. The blankets are packed in tightly, and they completely fill this small bin. In these days, the blankets are free of cooties. First guy on the plane. His seat is directly under the bin with the blankets. You can see this one coming. The guy now starts furiously throwing the blankets out of the bin so he can stow his bag in it. Either he's blind to all of the open space around him, or he is self-absorbed with single-minded purpose. I just don't get it. All of the other bins are empty! Now he can't reach the blankets that are jammed up against the back of the bin. If he stuffs his bag in there, we will never be able to get to those blankets if we need them. I offer to help, "Maybe we can move these out of the way so the passengers can get at them." I make no comment about the sheer idiocy of his actions. He sputters with indignation, "That's *just* what I'm *trying* to do!" I wouldn't be surprised if he exposed his fangs, or even if fire shot out of his eyes, right here and now. I need someone to shed light on this particular phenomenon, either from a passenger's point of view or a shrink's. Is it me, or is this guy missing lugnuts, wobbling off the road?

Flutes

We are sitting at the gate in Detroit waiting for our outbound. It's late and dark and we just want to get going. There's a man sitting across from us in a dim corner. He has long black hair, and he's playing one of those wooden flutes that reminds me of the Southwest. He closes his eyes, curls up into himself, and sways gently to the rhythm of his dark, haunting melody. Pan. I'm in a reverie. And then the agent hollers over to us that we can get on the plane now. Spell broken. The man playing the flute is on our flight. The flautist turns out to be an accomplished musician, and he's on his way to Pensacola for some engagement. He designs flutes by combining the best aspects of flutes ranging from Arizona to Africa, thus crafting completely new sounds. We talk about music for a while, and he gives us a little history lesson about how the flutes were used in ancient times. He shows us a little flute which he keeps in his pocket, a backup flute in case he needs an emergency flute fix. Then, he gives me one of his CDs. It is titled, "Atahualpa – Music from the Americas." Copyright 1999, Bolivar Burga.

Girl Learns to Walk

On this flight to Houston, there is a little girl with what I presume to be some sort of severe disability. She looks to be about four feet tall and maybe ten to twelve years old. She drools open-mouthed for the entire flight. I imagine the family grouping to be this: the girl, her grandparents, and her mother. The mother sits, staring vacantly into space. She isn't paying any attention to the girl at all. Her body language says, "Don't bother me." I'm not judging, just reporting. The grandparents seem to be doing most of the tending. The grandmother ambles the girl down the aisle, holding her frail arms aloft, while her floppy legs swing this way and that. When she was in her seat, the grandmother proudly told me that the girl just this week learned to walk. I congratulated the little girl on her success, but neither my comment nor my eyes were met with any response or recognition. I am having an emotional short-circuit, a little difficulty in processing what I'm witnessing. Young lady, ten years old, learns to walk. If anyone would complain to me in this moment about how hard their life is, I would want to smack them.

Girl Talk

There are things a man doesn't want to learn about a woman. For example, Suzy B. and Suzy Q. are talking. When they are at it, I sort of drift off and let it go—no sense in trying to stop a conversational cannonball. The topic on the van this morning is how they have both lost expensive jewelry that was given to them by their husbands, and how they had cheap copies made so they wouldn't have to tell. Their husbands wouldn't know the difference anyway.

Harry Potter

Abby, the other flight attendant, seems to be a sweet person—kind, generous and friendly—but she doesn't read *Harry Potter* books because her pastor said something about how they maybe weren't really all that good, on account of there being wizards and witches in them. I suggest to her that *Snow White* and *The Wizard of Oz* have witches and wizards. Witches can also be found in Greek mythology, Arthurian legends, and Grimm's fairy tales. Shakespeare. Not to mention, Samantha and Sabrina. Her pastor better get the word out on all that not-good stuff!

Heads

Heather gives the impression of being taller than she really is. I think of Joan Crawford. It is hard to determine exactly how tall Joan was, but she was not nearly as tall as she appeared to be in her films. Heather has that quality. Maybe it's her voice, maybe it's her swag or her piled-up hair or her heels. In fact, shoeless, she's no taller than I am, and I'm 5'6". She could be older than me, I think she looks older. I eventually find out that she's fifty-eight. She has grown kids with kids. Maybe it's her large head. She does have a large, round head. Sort of interesting, really. I got to examining her head shape once, and while she was talking to me all I heard was *blah blah blah*, because I was concentrating about how good her skull would be for a Yorick prop in *Hamlet*.

The other flight attendant is looking forward to a good steak in Omaha. He has a big, round, shiny bald head, and his specialty is sticking soda cans to it. A suction is created, and the can attaches itself. His head seems to have the right contours for can-sucking. He has said that with a little cooking oil, he can attach up to four cans. He is telling us how he preps his head, but all I hear is *blah blah blah*, because I'm concentrating on how stupid Yorick would look with Pepsi cans sucking at his skull.

(Google says Joan Crawford was 5'3".)

Help

Here's a flight attendant who thinks it's morally wrong to help people—not that I shouldn't help people, but that it is wrong to do so. I don't mind helping people with their bags, for example. I believe that's my job. On another occasion, when I went to get a wheelchair for a passenger who had been waiting and waiting, she had to tell me a convoluted story about a flight attendant who had done just that, slipped, fell, and got hurt, and the airline company got sued. I told her I wasn't going to slip. That sort of crap sounds crazy to me. She just doesn't want me making her look bad. I don't mind making her look bad, because she is. I wouldn't be writing this if that were all. On two of our first three flights, she failed to arm her doors after the announcement had been made. The pilots had to call back to remind her. Arming the door means to attach the raft/slide so that if the door is opened in an emergency, the raft will deploy and inflate. It is a standard, necessary procedure on all flights. When parked at the gate, the doors must then be disarmed. A flight attendant can be fired for failure to arm/disarm the door. On the second flight, her back galley was so insecure that on landing, sodas came flying out of the bustles, injuring her leg. This required an on-the-job-injury report. Five of the cans rocketed all the way up the aisle, shot through first class, and whacked up against the cockpit door. It wasn't only a matter of not helping people, it was a matter of not doing anything at all.

Hotel Tap Water

I'm talking about Maggie now, the lead flight attendant. I'd say she's direct. She'd say she's candid. If I say something she doesn't agree with, her eyes get all wide and white, her voice ratchets up a notch, and I think she expands—inflates—with righteous conviction. I was saying that I think the bottled water industry is largely a scam and that, for the most part, I just drink the water from the hotel room tap if it tastes ok. It can't kill me. Bam. Her eyes turn white, her hair shoots straight out like a shocked cat, her voice cranks up a couple of degrees on the Richter scale, and she lectures at me in a torrent of sentence beginnings, "Don't you know . . . Haven't you heard . . . Didn't you see on . . ." I have no recourse. I have to tell her that if there are no glasses in the hotel room, I'll just suck the water directly from the tap. I want to see if she'll puncture and whiz off into space. She is trying to tell me about some e-coli scare somewhere. When I ask her if anybody died, she isn't quite so certain. Maggie spends a good portion of our next day voicing her anxieties about the immediate future. "It's gonna be busy. I hope we have enough beverages, we can't give full cans. The Chicago flights are always full. We'll have to check bags. It's gonna be a hard flight to Tampa. I'm so tired, I hope it's a nice hotel. I hope it's not just a dump. We get there so late. It's probably half hour away, I hate those cheap sheets. I hope I can stay awake. The hotel could be a long way away, maybe I'll just sleep in the van. I hope the hotel isn't far away, they usually are on a long layover." So, I spend a good portion of my day with my mood shield at full glow. Sometimes I like to say things like, "Hey, Maggie, toss another squirrel on the grill, it looks like we're gonna be full," just to see. But, everything goes fine. Flights arrive on time. We have plenty of beverages. The hotel is five minutes away. The rooms are spacious. Sheets are fine. It's quiet.

Last day, Maggie is on her game. She's worrying about the weather. Her eyes are all big and white as she looks at the weather monitor and sees the yellow line we have to fly through. Yeah, yeah. "Through?" I'm thinking, "Over." As it happens, I'm glad she worries. The things she worries about don't seem to happen. She is sincere, though. Maybe by the end of the trip, I can teach her a little guile, you know, just a hint of craft. She needs to diversify her emotional portfolio. You can't have all of your character trait capital vested in sincerity. You have to learn how to fake sincerity.

Rachel, the other flight attendant, has pretty much drifted below my awareness horizon. She's there, she's nice, she's sweet, she's friendly. And she can say things like, "Wow," and, "Cool." Maggie and Rachel have so little in common, I hardly think they are even aware of each other. Rachel makes no comments or complaints about Maggie's lead style. She's wrapped up in a sincere effort to keep her galley clean and me at arm's length. Which is good.

So, I drift along out in the aisle, hand out my little blankies, flash my smile, and just let it all grind down toward layover. A woman even compliments me on my smile. I tell her I have an Academy Award for acting in a supporting role—one of my standard retorts. It takes her a moment.

Questions

"I have no idea!" is not the answer to the question, "What city is that down there? The correct answer is, "I don't know, but I will ask the captain, and maybe he can tell us."

The answer to the question, "What river is that down there?" is, "Snake."

Windshield

We are approaching Chicago after a long flight from Tokyo, maybe a couple of hours out. The captain comes on the P.A. and says, "Ladies and gentlemen, we have developed a mechanical problem that is going to cause us to divert and land in Minneapolis instead of Chicago. Ground personnel have been informed and will be making arrangements for your transfer to Chicago." It turns out that the right windshield has shattered. This is the window in front of the copilot, the first officer. The crackling is so severe that it has rendered the window opaque. We must divert to Minneapolis, where Northwest maintenance can repair the window, since aircraft with compromised windshields may not take off. The window itself is made up of more than one layer of material, and only one of those layers has cracked. If the whole window had blown, we'd all be dead. We flight attendants are allowed to enter the cockpit to see the damage, and I must say, it is a harrowing sight. It must have startled the first officer. He, someday, will sit in the captain's seat and will have this experience in his memory file. And, he will be able to advise his first officer, always, to pack extra underwear.

Old and Rude

• If I ever get so old and rude that I believe I am more important than others, please shoot me.

• If I ever get so old and rude that I believe I qualify for rights that others don't deserve, please shoot me.

• If I ever get so old and rude that I believe that rules are meant for others, not for me, please shoot me.

• If I ever get so old and rude that I don't need to listen to reasonable instructions, then please shoot me.

• If I ever get so old and rude that I prevent others from accomplishing their simple, necessary chores, please shoot me.

• If I ever get so old and rude that I believe a miracle has cured me and I no longer need the wheelchair I ordered, just shoot me.

• If I ever get so old and rude that I think if I just put on sunglasses, people will think I'm a celebrity, please just shoot me.

• If I ever get so old and rude that I treat the people who are kind to me like shit, don't hesitate, shoot me.

• If I ever get so old and obnoxious that I believe I can strike someone with my cane, just because I'm old, then, for God's sake, please shoot me. Now!

• And, if I ever get so old and rude and obnoxious that I forget that even old and rude and obnoxious people are still human beings and deserve to be treated with respect, well, strike me with a cane.

Inflatable Globe

For most of my years as an international flight attendant—flying often to Asia and beyond—I carried with me a small, inflatable globe. It weighed nearly nothing and took up hardly any space at all in my pocket. Fully inflated, it was about the size of a baseball. Because of its size, of necessity, it wasn't very detailed. But I took it with me for two reasons. For a demonstration, it answered the question of why we were flying over Alaska to get to Japan. It also answered the question, "Where are we now?" Imagine. We have been flying for seven hours on a thirteen-hour flight. We are still six hours from Japan. Looking out the plane window, you see nothing but an endless expanse of Pacific Ocean. Because we fly in total daylight, more or less keeping up with the sun, all of the window shades have been drawn to simulate night. I am monitoring the aisle when a passenger stirs, rubs his eyes, and through blurred awareness asks, "Where are we now?" I pull the flattened globe from my pocket, inflate it with two quick puffs, and point to a spot between a yellowish blotch labeled "U.S." and a tiny green fleck labeled "JPN." And for some reason, this would always strike me as funny—the passenger nods and says, "Oh."

July Fourth

I had a long flight on the night of July Fourth. The plane was nearly empty. I took a seat, looked down, and watched the U.S.A. drift by, all aglow with the sparkles of countless Independence Day celebrations. A rare sight, I believe, only ever seen by few. Now, there's a "snapshot."

Silver Dragon

It's morning here in Calgary. We all went out together to eat last night, the captain and three flight attendants. The copilot, fortunately for him, chose not to come with us. What a disaster! The night before, we meet at five in the lobby bar, and everybody but me has two drinks. I don't know how many drinks were consumed in the room before coming to the lobby. I'm hoping nobody lights a match. Four people are deciding where to go to eat. Jennifer has a taste for Chinese. "There's a Chinese restaurant right across the street." That turns out to be just a sushi bar. I could go for beef, since there's a steak house right next door. In five minutes, my hand could be wrapped around a Labatt Blue, but Jennifer, who is wearing blinders to anyone else's suggestions, has unilaterally decided on China. She asks the concierge where there would be a good Chinese restaurant. We're in luck, I guess, because Chinatown is only three blocks away. The concierge recommends the Silver Dragon. Already, I'm not liking this. It's twenty-eight degrees outside, and I don't have Canadian weather-wear. So now we have to have the obligatory discussion about whether we really want Chinese or not. Jennifer doesn't want steak. Everybody is trying to be patient and accommodating, but the die had been cast a long time ago: China. The directions to the Silver Dragon are as simple as can be—three blocks down, turn left. Of course, nobody listens. We turn left after two blocks and stand on the corner shivering in the cold, bewildered. Jennifer has to go to the bathroom, so as long as we don't know where we're going, let's run there. We are loping into Chinatown looking for the Silver Dragon.

"Those are Americans," I hear a mother explain to her child as we jog along.

We run past a veritable cornucopia of quaint little Chinese places. No dice. Silver Dragon. We find the Silver Dragon and of course, it's upscale. Why wouldn't it be? It was recommended by the Westin. A huge, smiling Buddha statue greets us as we enter—a harbinger of what I expect to look like when we leave. The menu has so many pages of selections, I fear I'll die of malnutrition before I get to the end. I feel skeletal. Jennifer, ever the conductor of this mayhem, wants everybody to get something different and then share. She wants tofu. Diane says she doesn't eat tofu. So, Jennifer's plan is shot down right away. On the last page, I see a special meal for four. That seems to be a good plan, and everybody agrees to that. It will be a feast of dizzying variety. But when the food starts coming—you know, the wonton soup, the spring roll, the tea—my poor gut is already bursting. I feel more Buddha-ish than skeletal. I have a splitting headache. The beef and broccoli, the sweet and sour chicken, the mushrooms, the sprouts, the water chestnuts, the rice, the pork, the shrimp—all that is still to come. All I want is to be back in my room.

On returning to the hotel, Jennifer has to go to the bathroom again, so at least we can run. Like Americans

Jer-ry

According to some, I bear a resemblance to Jerry Springer. So this kid on the plane is yelling "Jer-ry, Jer-ry, Jer-ry!" every time I go past him in the aisle. What is the kid's mother thinking? It's amazing what parents will let their kids reveal about them.

Jesus Speaks

Rodney tells the story of a flight attendant who came to work late with the excuse that Jesus had told her she should sleep in a little bit so she would be well-rested for the passengers. Rodney asked if she was sure that it wasn't the devil who told her to sleep late and was only disguising himself as Jesus, because that is what the devil does to get flight attendants into trouble.

Rodney tells me another story about a flight attendant who doesn't serve milk—a hard and fast general rule from her personal rule supply. Not for babies, not for children, not for coffee, not at all. Doesn't matter how much milk there is on hand or how much might be wasted.

I would happily read Rodney's collection of flight attendant "snapshots."

Just This Flight

A passenger is dressed all in blue. The guy is about my height, and his blue suit is roughly the color of a '92 Corsica. Blue pinstripe pants, blue vest, blue sport jacket, blue and white striped tie, powder blue shirt, and a blue top hat. A blue top hat! Now that's a sight.

Then we have the nester. This little girl is *so* cute. She is snuggled up with her little Sierra Mist and her little blankie and a big bag of sunflower seeds, and she has created a pile of sunflower husks on the floor under her seat by the time the flight is over.

Finally, after we are parked at the gate, a man in the last row goes into the lav, I guess, just to blow his nose. *Omigod!* People three and four rows up from the lav can hear these snorts! He sounds like an old model car trying to start up in cold weather. Everybody is laughing. His wife is in tears. When he comes out, with a sheepish grin on his face, he must be realizing that his volcanic eruptions had been heard. I say to him, "Well, we were planning on repainting the lav anyway." That gets another round of laughter—from the culprit, as well.

Food and Water

Here is a flight attendant who's fussy about what she eats. She likes to remind everyone (whether they are seeking reminding or not) that there are 15,000 chemicals in the foods we consume. So, she eats only kosher meat. I ask her if she is sure it isn't maybe only 14,999. No, she's sure.

Another flight attendant is a water freak. He carries water with him all the time, forever sipping from his personal water container, even if he is in the aisle in the middle of his service. He is constantly advocating the virtues of being and staying "hydrated." He tells me that if I drink when I am thirsty, it's too late! When I scoff, he is unable to explain "too late."

There have been times in my life when I have been thirsty, and I have probably consumed my share of chemicals. However, I am nearly sixty and am neither dried out nor suffering from a chemical imbalance. And I don't try to fix other people.

Lav Doors

I have a more patient attitude toward passengers who are unable to get into the lav than most flight attendants. Most people are not required to read a door, any door, as they approach it. This is necessary on the Airbus. A plaque on the door says *"Push."* And, most doors don't crease in the middle and fold inward when they open. Those on the Airbus do. Most doors have a handle or a knob. On the Airbus, not. A typical image is this: Passenger approaches the lav door, stares blankly at it, maybe reaches for the ashtray, thinking it's the door handle and here is where the flight attendant puts her magazine down, rolls his or her eyes, and thinks, *"Gawd, can't you read?"* If I'm there, I just push the door inward for them.

Having said that, I've never had so many people unable to figure out how to get into the lav. One guy pinched his fingers. Another person wasn't expecting the door to fold inward, so she lost her balance and nearly fell into the lav. I know I've said that it's not the passengers' job to know these things, but today there seemed to be an epidemic of people struggling with the lav doors. I'm not proud of this, but at one point I rolled my eyes and said, "Good Gawd, what is wrong with people? Can't they read?"

Red Socks

Not pertaining to anything, and for no reason, I have never cared much for the Christmas carol, "Feliz Navidad." And how that ever became part of Debbie's awareness, I cannot remember. In Minneapolis, on our layover, we part ways. She goes to the mall and, while there, buys for me a pair of red socks with an image of a cactus and the words "Feliz Navidad" on them. She gets a greater pleasure out of this than I do. But, for a joke, on our flight to Hartford, I wear these gaudy, red outrages. I thought she was never going to stop laughing. She says that if the socks had cost fifty dollars, it would have been worth it. I say, "Please, Debbie, I'm worth more than that!" They are not good socks. They make my feet hot and itchy, and they will be in the next box of stuff we take to Goodwill.

Snail

Here's a joke. A guy finds a snail on his front stoop. He picks it up and throws it across the street. One year later, he hears a knock at the door. The guy goes to the door, opens it, looks down, and there he sees the snail back on his front stoop. And the snail looks up at the guy and says, "What the hell was that all about?"

The captain, the first officer, Jan and I are at a restaurant on our layover, eating pizza. Jan and I have very little in common with the German pilot (who hasn't been to Germany in years) and the Italian first officer (who is God's gift to humanity). So, the conversation devolves to jokes. When I tell the snail joke, Germany and Italy just don't get it, mimicking in some way the punch line of the joke. Blank looks. But Jan is dissolving into uncontrollable spasms of laughter. Our hotel is only about four blocks away, and as we walk back, Jan is laughing for three of them. Every now and then, she mumbles a phrase or two from the joke to herself and then starts up laughing all over again. In the morning, we gather in the hotel lobby for our van ride to the airport. I see Jan coming out of the elevator. She sees me and erupts once more in laughter. Best response to a joke I ever told.

Ed

Ed McMahon is on our flight to Winnipeg. At some point, I say to him, "Having you with us tonight will give me something to tell my wife when I email her tonight." He says, "That is very nice," and he offers me his hand. (I know, it's not much, but you work with what you've got.)

Bart

Bart Starr is on our flight from Birmingham to Detroit. Once he gets settled in his seat, I approach him and say, "If you are not Bart Starr, you sure look like him." This seems to delight him. He stands up, smiles, and shakes my hand. And at the cost of not being too forward, he offers to send me a signed photo. Now *I* am delighted. He takes down my name and address, and now, I am the owner of a beautiful, 8x10, color, personalized action photo of Bart Starr. And, a kind, signed letter. It didn't occur to me to ask him if he was related to Ringo.

Confused?

We served an embarrassingly small package of a sandwich (it might have been turkey or ham) with carrots, which were suitable for a Peyronie's disease ad. When a passenger asks me about the sandwich, I tell her I think it's the mouseloaf. Personally, I prefer the goat-eyeball sandwich, because I like the squirt when you bite down.

Then, there's a woman who has lost her luggage. It is a black tote, and it isn't where she stowed it. We open up nearly all of the bins helping her look for it. Well, it turns out to be in the bin right above her seat! It isn't black. It's blue. She actually has to open it to make sure it is hers. I don't know why she was so confused. Maybe she ate something that disagreed with her. Mouseloaf?

FAA Agents

In my entire career, I was never tested or questioned by any FAA (Federal Aviation) official. Nevertheless, this was always a concern. They, according to the rumors, were able to question flight attendants on all sorts of safety issues, verify adherence to procedures, and have you point out pages in your huge flight attendant manual that applied to various concerns, which were many, varied and impossible to memorize (that's why we have pre-flight briefings). If FAA agents were ever onboard, they went to the cockpit, and I hardly ever even saw them.

Now we go to door three, aircraft right, Boeing 757. I am sitting at my jump seat, facing aft. Across from me in seats D, E, and F are three young men. They appear to be healthy and capable. Since they are sitting at an exit row, I have given them an extra briefing on the operation of the door. They are expected to help in case of an emergency. They would have been denied exit row seating if they had refused those responsibilities. By and large, these are good seats with plenty of legroom. Nevertheless, they are a bit cramped, and it is a long flight. It is for this reason that I allow the man at the E (center) seat to sit on my jump seat for a while. I brief him. If anything unexpected should occur, he is to return to his assigned seat. He understands. This now allows the other two men in that row to catch a breather. Sometimes when you do one favor, there are collateral beneficiaries. From my point of view, no safety concern has been compromised. He is one step away from his seat, and he has been briefed. Still though, this does not go well with another flight attendant. She is, like, scandalized. "You know, Phil, if FAA is onboard, you can be fired." It doesn't please her that I go, "Yeah, yeah." So, she elevates it into the crazy zone. "And if there are two FAA agents onboard and one of them does not fire you, the second one can fire the first one for not firing you." She actually says that. I say, "Yeah, if."

Apple Juice

I am standing, facing the corner of the aft galley. Any person coming into the galley will see my back. In my hand, I have a can of apple juice. On the floor between my spread legs is a plastic cup. If I slowly pour a stream of apple juice into the cup, from behind it looks like I'm taking a leak. That's the setup for when Angela comes to the galley. Tom gives me the signal that Angela is coming, and I start "peeing." Angela is aghast for a moment. Now she sees the joke and laughs. But then, I pick up the cup, swirl it around a bit, and say, "Looks a little cloudy. I'll pass it through again." And then I drink it.

Trixie

We've just started our beverage service in the main cabin when a passenger asks Trixie (who might just as well have been named "Stormy" or "Bubbles") for a blanket. She turns and looks at me wide-eyed and mouths the words, "Oh my gawd!" This embarrasses me. I don't think anyone saw her mouth the words, but I can feel the pink rise up in my cheeks. What is the passenger supposed to do? Sit and shiver until it's convenient for the flight attendant—which may be never! You'd think Trixie had been asked for a severed finger or a mummified monkey paw. Generally speaking, Trixie is not in the flight. She's in some realm of awareness that has excluded her job, her responsibilities, and her colleagues. She's not around to close the galley cart doors or the bustle doors as a safety requirement for landing. She is rarely available for routine monitoring of the aisles. She does her service and then buries her snoot in a magazine. The plane could blow up, and she'd be found on the ground with her blown-off nose snot-glued to a lipstick ad. I am not her "new best friend." I'd rather have a week's worth of used cat litter for a friend. Whew, I feel better now.

Make that Bud Light (-en up)

There are over 8 billion individuals living on earth. Earth is one of the smaller planets and is part of a system of eight or so planets whirling about our nearest star neighbor, the sun. The sun, an ordinary star, is located in a rather ordinary corner of an ordinary star system known as the Milky Way galaxy. The Milky Way is composed of 100 billion or more such stars and extends its gossamer, crystalline arms across a space so vast that even at the speed of light, it would take 100 thousand years just to traverse its diameter (not counting rush hour or coffee breaks). The Milky Way galaxy, however, is just one of more than a hundred billion known galaxies that spin their ancient dance across the vast arc of the universe. The distances between objects, the unremittingly imposing omnipresence of space itself, renders null the notion of substance: for all practical purposes, there is nothing there! When one considers all of this, when one ponders the exquisite texture, the lush radiance of our celestial habitat, it does seem inappropriate that you would get outraged because a passenger asks for wine at breakfast-time or a blanket during your service or, for heaven sakes, another bag of pretzels.

I'm talking to you, Trixie. And you, too, Bob.

Wet Seat

We started out a little bit delayed because a guy had a wet seat cushion, and we needed to get him a fresh one. At first, he was really mad, stormed around for a little bit, and after we got his cushion exchanged, it turned out that the seatbelts were all wet, too. Replacing seat belts is a different story. We can easily change a wet seat cushion for a dry one, but we need a mechanic to replace a seat belt. We knew and he knew, of course, that it was only water, or rather, some ice that had spilled on the seat. As the delay got longer and longer, his cloudy temperament turned sunnier. Pretty soon, he was almost apologetic. "After all, it's only a little water. I'm ok. We don't need to delay because of this," and so on. It's too late, of course. Once you start a procedure involving mechanics, there's paperwork that has to be completed and then signed off. When flight attendants are dreading the upcoming, slowly diminishing, already short layover, the most dreaded word is "mechanical." Those are long, long minutes.

Denise

Denise can really talk. At least she talks fast. On the van ride from the hotel to the airport this morning, she kept up such a nonstop rhythmic patter of inconsequential material that we were pretty much asleep again before we had even started work. Sue and I defer the lead position to Denise. I serve drinks to passengers in first class during the boarding. When a man requests a decaf, I brew some and serve it to him. This disturbs Denise. The passenger should have waited until after takeoff for his coffee. It's such a waste for the company. It is so upsetting to her aura. Her *aura!* Yeah, and I have an aura, too. But I left it in my luggage for this trip so whenever she talks, it won't blow away. The service is so simple: if I can do it, I do it. The pouch of decaf was going to be used, one way or another, before or after takeoff. Later, on our next flight to Missoula, the first person in first class wants, of course, a decaf. I'm not going to argue with Denise (or upset her aura). I just go to the back galley and get him a cup. When Denise wonders why I went to the back, I tell her. She bellows, "You are bloody kidding." The passenger can hear this. I can hear her aura screaming. It's all kind of funny, in a way. But sometimes I dread those flights with a light passenger load. Just the setting for the old adage of what can happen, namely: shit.

Wheelchair

We have a wounded soldier onboard. He has no legs below the knees. His own wheelchair is in the belly of the aircraft. On arrival at the gate, baggage handlers will bring his wheelchair up to the jetway, so it is available as soon as he gets off. There are people in the jetway now waiting for the deplaning to begin. An elderly man gets off the plane. His son is in the jetway, waiting. A wheelchair would be useful. So, the son puts his dad in the soldier's wheelchair, and off he goes. It's going to be a while before anyone realizes what has happened. In fact, I invented the scenario. Something like that must have happened. The soldier is not happy. In fact, he is livid. In my career, I have never experienced any passenger who, for any reason, was as blisteringly angry as this soldier. Maybe, rightfully so. But he is yelling and cursing and damning innocent people and spouting all kinds of profanities. "Goddammit, there are laws in Washington D.C. to prevent this sort of shit from happening!" Not true. It was an accident, an oversight. Regrettable, yes, but not malicious. No one seems to be capable of imagination, except for Cindy and me. Where could this wheelchair have gone? Well, probably to baggage claim. So, together and off the clock, we start the long trek to baggage claim. On the way, we see the wheelchair—empty, coming back toward us. It seems as though someone recognized that this was tagged as a personal wheelchair and was single-mindedly bringing it back to the gate. Cindy and I take over and roll the chair as quickly as we can back to the waiting soldier. The soldier somehow mistakenly thinks that we are the cause of his problem and is less than grateful. I'll just say, we are not thanked for our service.

Leather Face

A man comments on the fact that at the end of the flight, I am still smiling. A little, leathery-faced old hag sitting behind him cackles out, "He has to smile, that's his job." "No, lady, smiling is not my job. Biting my tongue and stifling my giggles is my job, because you are such a sideshow freak," is what I don't say.

On this flight, we had a variety of pukers. One of them up in first class got kind of messy. And then there was another one at landing, and she handed it to me already in the barf-bag. Then there was this sticky turd that clung tenaciously to the side of the toilet bowl. God, it was just a short flight with only a beverage service, but somehow it seemed a lot longer.

Smile

A flight attendant does not particularly like to be told to smile. Flight attendants are service and safety professionals doing their job. Sure, it is nice to smile. It would be nice if your plumber or your auto mechanic would smile, too. But we don't wonder of them, "Why the long face?" I'm sitting at the back of the 727 on the aft-facing jump seat during taxi. My face is at rest. I am not angry or sullen or defeated. So, when the passenger sitting across the aisle from me leans over and tells me to "lighten up," I laugh out loud. If he is in the habit of judging a person's emotional state by evaluating facial contours, he sure has picked the wrong guy to practice on. I tell him, "I am over forty years old. I have been flying for only a couple of years now, and when Northwest Airlines hired me, my dream came true. This job suits me. In fact, I was just thinking about how much I love this job. And oh, by the way, have you seen the female flight attendants I get to work with? And you think I'm darkened down? I was just taking these moments to reset my face, because it is always so stretched out of shape from grinning." I think he realizes that I don't need any "lightening up." He smiles.

Crop-Dusting

When I was a child, I learned to make fart sounds with my hands and mouth. For example, if you blow into your hand at the V where your thumb and forefinger meet, you can create squeaky, high-pitched fart sounds. If you blow into the center cup of your hand, you get the deeper, more resonant raspberries. I can also make fart sounds by releasing, in a burst, the suction from trapped air when both my hands are pressed together. That one will sound a bit like an animated cartoon kiss. Smack! I am an adult now and, as such, get scant pleasure out of farts, farting, or fart-like noises. Right. Farts are, nevertheless, funny. Farts are their own punchline. For example: You are at the dentist, and he is busy drilling out a cavity. A nurse walking by in the hall farts. You and dentist both hear this unmistakable piercing rupture of sound. Ten tear-filled minutes later, you and your dentist are able, with seriously stressed ribs, to continue with the appointment. True story. See, no long buildup. Fart = punchline. The original laughing gas. Farts, of course, are a routine aspect of airline travel. Passengers are constantly releasing their internal fumes and fragrances into the fragile aircraft atmosphere. This often becomes hilariously, as well as painfully evident to the surrounding fellow travelers. Now, when you see a female flight attendant floating down the aisle going nowhere wearing a cherubic smile on her face, you may be sure she is "crop-dusting." If you do not know what "crop-dusting" is, I assume that from the topic at hand, now you do know. I use a female flight attendant as an example because, as everyone knows, a man has no interest in farts or farting. It provides for them little or no amusement.

Robert

Early in my career, I met a young flight attendant, whom I shall call Robert. Both of us, based in Detroit, were of approximately similar seniority. So it happened that when we coincidentally parallel bid, we got scheduled on the same trip several times. Robert came across as a quiet flight attendant with a kind soul, but it was his wonderful sense of humor that beguiled me as I got to know him better. He could say simple, dry things that would leave me weak and sore. He must have enjoyed my sense of humor too, because one day he invited me to his home for an overnight. And I accepted. We spent the day visiting a museum or two, seeing some of the local sights and having ribs at Corky's. The next day, as I was getting ready for my flight, Robert explained to me that the gate agents at the airport were very strict about employee pass-travel attire, so he loaned me his sport jacket, just so there wouldn't be any problems.

Time passes. I transfer to the Chicago base, and Robert falls beneath my radar. When I next see Robert, he is a woman! Still, as far as I can tell, she is the same person he had always been, with maybe a bit more glow. You see, Robert was born with two complete sets of sexual organs. At birth, Robert's father decided to allow the doctor to favor the male. Wrong choice. Robert did not know of this until his twenties, when during a routine medical checkup, the doctor made this discovery. As for Robert, however, vague, blurry questions about his own orientations came suddenly into sharp focus. It was as if a curtain had been pulled back or, in fact, had abruptly collapsed. For years, it may be that Robert lived in his own skin as an alien. Robert did not have a sex change. She always was a woman, and being able to actually live like one must have been a bit like becoming native, becoming yourself, or going home. Wouldn't it be a wonderful, beautiful thing if all those who have similar heartbreaking yearnings would be able, like Robert and like E.T., to go home?

Fear of Flying

Most fear of flying, I believe, comes from passengers' discomfort with turbulence. Or, a vague sense that things up in the air should fall, that a plane will somehow just drop out of the sky or crash. I understand this feeling. True story: I traveled to Europe and back by ship two times (twice!) because of my uneasiness about flying. At some point, it came to me that being a flight attendant would suit my idea of the perfect job. So, I either give up a dream or give up a fear. Here are some of the things I say to passengers who exhibit fear of flying. This aircraft is designed to fly. It is engineered to fly. It is meant to fly. Flying is what is does, what it is meant to do. In the air, free of gravity, is where the plane lives, where the plane loves to be and is at home. Pilots and flight attendants feel this in a profound way. In fact, when you are on an American airplane, it is quite possible that you are in one of the safest environments on the planet. Imagine a swan on land, waddling clumsily toward the shore. Now the swan is in the water, calm and serene. Like an airplane, slow and clumsy on earth, but a reigning queen of the sky. The plane has two major requirements: wings and air. Air rushing under the wings gives the plane life. It doesn't matter if the air is bumpy. It is still air. "Consider this image: a cork floating on the river can pass through the rapids and still will not sink."

Compressor Stall

A compressor stall is a phenomenon that occurs during the takeoff where the engine does not get quite enough air and it chokes or backfires. Typically, it is because of crosswinds on the runway. To the passenger, it sounds like an explosion and can be quite frightening, although there is little, if any, danger. Depending on the circumstances, the pilot will choose either to go ahead and take off, or to abort and try again. He or she will almost always make an announcement. Until that moment, it can be hard to relax. Due to modern engineering and the sophistication of current designs, compressor stalls are nearly nonexistent. I flew on a number of DC-9s and Boeing 727s (which are probably no longer in service) and after having "survived" my first stall (and refreshing my underwear), I was able, immediately, to reassure passengers when it happened again.

Kidney

We are in Minneapolis, waiting for our last flight of the day to Chicago. It's late, and we are going to be delayed because of the weather. We're groaning because our Chicago layover is already built at near minimum, so we're dreading delaying the Chicago outbound in the morning for legal rest reasons. If you know the night before that you are going to begin your next day behind schedule, automatically, that will be a bad day. In short, you will be tired, and your passengers will be crabby. It will be all about 'connections.' It can affect the whole day. Bad weather doesn't necessarily stop air traffic, but it can slow it down. There are exceptions. In fact, as luck would have it, shortly before our scheduled departure time, we suddenly learn that we will be transporting kidneys to Chicago. This is an urgent matter. We board the plane quickly, we roll down the tarmac, we curl without stopping onto the runway, we take off and arrive in Chicago fifteen minutes early! It's good they weren't my kidneys though. I was so excited to arrive early that I nearly wet my pants.

Pineapple

A woman boards the plane with her hair piled so high upon her head that it reminds me of a pineapple. She sits in first class at 3A. I am helping the lead flight attendant serve drinks to the first-class passengers. Toward the end of the boarding process, Marcus, the other flight attendant, comes up into first class. I say to him, "Marcus, look around first class and tell me if you see any fruit." He takes a quick look around and without hesitation says, "3A pineapple." I understand that reading this might not seem so hilarious as having experienced it.

Birds

Many people don't know the difference between a direct flight and a nonstop flight. A nonstop flight actually has one stop... the one when you arrive. A direct flight can have one or more landings before you get to your destination. For example, a direct flight from Milwaukee to New Orleans may stop in Memphis. Although the flight number will not change, it is possible that you will have to get off in Memphis and proceed to another gate. When this happens, as it often does, it can be confusing, especially for people with disabilities who may have been told in Milwaukee that there would be no plane change. It is less hard on the crew, because one crew may have finished their day and will be getting off in Memphis anyway, while a new crew will continue with the passengers on to New Orleans. The passengers, if they are lucky, will be informed before they arrive in Memphis that there will be a plane change. If there is no plane change, the passengers are free to remain on the plane, or, if the stopover is lengthy, to deplane and relax in the relative comfort of the terminal and await reboarding. The length of the stopover is iffy. It can be thirty minutes or an hour and a half. And the above phrase, "if they are lucky" will soon come into focus.

I am working a flight from Las Vegas to Detroit. This is a direct flight continuing to Cleveland. There is no indication that there will be a plane change in Detroit for those who are Cleveland-bound. For me, this is the last flight of the day and of the trip. I have long-since booked a seat for myself on my commuter flight home to Milwaukee. I am hoping everything is on time, since it is a fairly tight connection. If I don't make my connection, I may have to spend the night in Detroit and fly home on the next flight to Milwaukee in the morning. We are on time and since the flight to Cleveland will depart about an hour later, all of the passengers, including the Cleveland passengers, deplane. We, the flight attendants, are the last to get off, and as we prepare to scurry to our respective commuter flights, the gate agent informs us that there has been an unscheduled plane change. *So what?* I'll tell you so what! We are now enlisted to go back on the plane and remove the luggage left onboard by the through-passengers, the passengers who were thinking (and were told) that this was their plane to Cleveland. This is particularly irritating, because the time spent hauling luggage off the plane could cause us to miss our commuter flights. And it is just goodwill, because it is completely off the clock. It is going well, there is not much through-luggage. There will be time, after all, to catch my flight. While we are busily flitting around making sure that the aircraft is free of passenger carry-ons, I notice a shoebox under one of the seats. Some tiny holes have been poked into the lid of the shoebox. It may just be garbage. I open it and am startled to see that it is full of tiny, animated birds. Before I can get the lid back on, three of the birds manage to escape and fly about the cabin. You can imagine the ensuing scene: Three flight attendants are chasing three tiny (probably terrified) birds around the interior of an Airbus. I missed that page in my job description. We develop a plan. First, close the aircraft door, so the birds don't utterly escape. Second, scare them into flying into a smaller space...the cockpit. This being done, we are able to trap them in the angled wedge of the cockpit window and return them briskly into their shoebox.

And that really is the end of the story. We never hear another word about the birds, who owned them, or what purpose they had in Cleveland. Or even if they had names, like Chick, Jay, Rob or Ladybird. Middles of stories. We even suspect that something illegal might have been going on. In the end, I am able to hurry to my gate and watch as my flight home departs, without me.

Throws Up

Here we have an unaccompanied minor—a polite little boy so nattily dressed he could be a miniature business man, or maybe a Mensa candidate who speaks four languages and has memorized the New Testament, in Hebrew. He is going to Dallas to visit his grandparents for a week. Now, I am working in the main cabin, so I escort him to his seat and give him his little personal briefing—where the exits are, how to use the O2 masks, don't leave the plane without us, and blah, blah. Kathy, the lead flight attendant, has already introduced me to him. She said, "This is John, he throws up." And so he does. We give him some of our gray trash pickup bags, and every now and then I get a glimpse of his little head, stuck discreetly half in the bag, barfing like a sailor on shore leave. Toward the end of the flight, we go to the medical kit and dig out a red biohazard bag so the cleaners can handle it with the necessary precautions. It's hardly necessary. Little John is so fastidious that there is not a speck of barf anywhere, except, I presume, inside the bag. He even wraps up the gray bags by himself, inserts them in the red biohazard bag, and otherwise follows our instructions precisely. I feel a little bad for the man in the middle seat sitting next to little John, having to listen to a child puke for two hours, so I give him a couple of beers, and he is very nice. In fact, he probably has projectile vomit kids of his own, but he just doesn't get free beer when they vomit projectile-ly. And on the very next flight, back from Dallas to Detroit, we have another "little John" that pukes. I don't think that is part of his identity, though. He is just sick.

Ruszcyk

There's a flight attendant whose name is Mary Ruszcyk. I say to her, "How do you pronounce your name, again?" She says, "Ruzz-check." I say, "No, I mean your first name."

Michael Bolton

Michael Bolton is sitting in first class on his way to New York. He has finished his drink, and I've cleared away his glass. The plane starts to push back, and we begin our safety demos. He interrupts me during my safety demo by poking at my elbow to point at the cup from the passenger sitting next to him. It needs to be removed. Mike, relax. I'll take care of it. I've flown for twenty-one years, and no passenger has ever poked at me as a reminder to remove an empty glass. Ever. So, Michael Bolton and I have this thing in common that we share with no one else in the entire universe. And, more important, I am as good a flight attendant as he is a singer. I may be better, because I've never poked him and said, "You're a little pitchy."

Computer Jerk

The doors are armed, the bins are closed, the passengers are seated with tray tables up, and all luggage is stowed. We are taxiing in Detroit for takeoff to Saginaw. Oops! I notice a man with his tray table down and his computer still illuminated. I say to him, "You'll need to stow your computer now." There is no hint of impatience or even annoyance in my tone. Fine, he honors my instruction and stows his computer. Now, because of fog in Saginaw, we are held up on the tarmac in Detroit. This guy, without permission, gets out his computer again. What do I do? Well, I call the pilot and ask him if he knows when we'll depart and if it's ok if this guy uses his computer. The pilot says that the minimums are lifting in Saginaw, that we should be departing soon, and that he would prefer it if the guy turns his computer off. I go to the guy and tell him that I just conferred with the pilot about his computer, and the pilot said that since we are expecting to depart soon, he'd prefer it if the computer were off. The guy says to me, "Well, that was a lot nicer than when you told me to turn it off before." I start to say that I certainly didn't mean to come across as unfriendly or impolite, but he waves me off and interrupts my sentence by saying, "Doesn't matter." He waves me off! Wow!

There's a lot to unpack here. 1) He was in violation of a federal regulation. Period. It is my duty to enforce his compliance. He has to know this. He must comply for two reasons: A) The use of electronic devices is considered a safety concern, and B) His noncompliance, if unaddressed, sends a message to the other passengers that it is ok to ignore safety regulations. 2) He doesn't seem to realize that his disruptive behavior has been graciously tolerated by the crew. What he should have said, instead of, "Doesn't matter," is, "Thank you for letting me know." But he is "special." 3) It is a personal insult. He can wave *me* off, but he will accept the authority of the *pilot*. It is very unlikely that he will be thrown off the plane or met by the law in Saginaw. Those are possible but remote possibilities. That is up to him. Turns out, it *does* matter. Strange, though—during the flight itself, his computer remains stowed. He doesn't use it at all.

Crowne Plaza

Bob, Larry, and Phil waiting for their lunch at Crowne Plaza.

Beryllium

For boarding, the cockpit door is open. A passenger often sticks his head in just to greet the pilot or say hi. This time, the copilot (the first officer) is not present, and the passenger wants to know where he is. I never tire of saying, "We are a little low on beryllium beads, and he has gone off to see if can get some more. That's what keeps us up in the air, you know." After an appropriate pause for effect, I explain that the first officer is making his checklist rounds. He must go outside the aircraft and examine the listed aspects of its exterior. We don't go if this isn't done. More than one passenger enjoys the joke, though.

Three-Part Joke

I can hardly remember where we came from or where we are going in this story. It is late, and we have an unscheduled aircraft and gate change. We are tired, and our last flight of the day will be somewhere close, like Detroit to Kalamazoo. The people-mover in Detroit is out of order, and our new gate is at the far end of the terminal. We, as you may have guessed, are at the other far end. This seems to be a rule when you are already nearly spent. We will walk a mile, Brittany in her concourse heels, all of us dragging our roller bags along. We will not stop at Taco Bell for a Crunchwrap. We will not pause to relieve our bladders. The continuing passengers who are on this flight with us must make this mile-long trek, too. Since this is a direct flight and the passengers were not told in advance about these changes, they are not happy. It will take us fifteen to twenty minutes to get there, down the long, now dimmed concourse.

This is when Douglas chooses to tell us one of his "famous" three-part jokes. You know the kind. You groan, because generally they are not very funny. The reason they call it a punchline is because by the time you get to it, you're punchy. And, I can hardly hear Douglas. He talks fast and I can't look at him, because I'm purposefully marching forward with my eyes glued to the horizon. And it's partly because I'm not listening. This joke goes on for nearly the duration of our walk. When he finally says, "Put a rubber on the pickle," I laugh politely. He is laughing so broadly—as if he has just heard the joke, not told it—that he doesn't notice me not responding in the way he might have hoped.

The passengers who have preceded us to that far, lonely gate applaud with derision as we approach. It's just a handful. Maybe they think we're responsible for this delay and inconvenience. Maybe it's not derision. Maybe it's relief. Maybe, maybe, maybe. Here's a three-part joke: Delay, deride and depart. One dark night in Detroit, three verbs are trying to get to Kalamazoo (AZO). The "delay" just can't get going because all the people have to walk a mile first. The "deride" is pissed because the delay was on account of a tenacious turd in the toilet basin that clogged up the line. The "depart" is the punchline. Who knew that departing for AZO at midnight, spent and hungry, could be so funny?

Omaha

It is early morning, and I am alone in the lobby of the hotel. When the other crew members come down from their rooms, the driver of the hotel van will take us to the airport. The bright lights seem to make the still lobby even more silent. There are no windows. The night manager has nothing to do, so he stands looking vacantly at the wall, asleep with open eyes. I, too, am staring at the wall. A moment or two of just nothing passes.

Afterwards, I recall that in that sheer moment, I had lost all sense of awareness. I might have flickered and disappeared, leaving behind a couple of faint sparkles. Not even a random thought. The lobby itself offered no point of interest, and for that moment I lost any sense of where or even who I was. Just tuned out, turned off. I suspect that other flight attendants have similar moments, what with time zone changes and erratic sleep schedules. Poor nutrition, personal hygiene challenges, separation anxieties . . .

The Woman at the Window

I am in Singapore at a busy intersection about to cross the street. To my left, a bus is also waiting for the light to turn green. When it does, I step off the curb and look up to see the bus rolling by. There is a woman in the bus with her palms flat against the window looking right at me. Our eyes lock for an electric moment. And then the bus rumbles on. If this scene had been in a movie, the audience might have shivered slightly, recognizing this moment as a portent of some future significance. It was, of course, nothing of the sort. It wasn't a movie, just a coincidence.

But I ponder the random curiosities of space and time that brought us (me and the woman in the bus window) together at that precise instant. A second or two, a step or two, a tiny ripple in the flow of time and this meeting would never have occurred. There are some who like to say that there is a reason for everything. They are wrong. This event fell outside of any discernable continuum. It was purposeless coincidence. Everything is coincidence. Everything!

And then, I continue on my way to the Singapore Crocodile Farm.

Airplane

Airlines: What goes up, must come down. Airline food: What goes down, must come up.

Mixed Nuts

I'm serving drinks in first class. As I serve a drink, I lay on the tray table a bag of pretzels and a bag of mixed nuts. "Mixed nuts" is an apt metaphor for the first-class passengers today. This "nut," without comment, tosses his bag of mixed nuts back up onto my cart. What would you think? I think he doesn't want the mixed nuts. Many people do return things, though they usually say something, like, "No thanks," or "I don't eat nuts," or... anything. That he just tossed them back on my cart is not the problem. The problem is that when I pick them up and put them back in the drawer, he says, "I wouldn't put those back in the drawer if I were you." I'm still not getting it. Then I see that the nut bag is soiled. (Whoa there, another metaphor alert). What does he think I'm supposed to think? I need for him to say something. I never read *Mind Reading for Dummies*. So, I give him an unsoiled bag of nuts and he thanks me. But put yourself in a similar position. Wouldn't you have said something, like, "There's lipstick on this glass," or "There's a fly in my soup." I guess there's a book he hasn't read: *Common Courtesies for Dummies*. The image of James Cagney saying, "You dirty nut bag," keeps me on kilter for the rest of the flight.

Bag Move

We're delayed out of Detroit, and there is a man sitting in the last row who is concerned about his connection in Houston. I offer to move him to the front of the plane so he can get off more quickly. There are many open seats in the first few rows of the main cabin. He can have his choice. His carry-on bag is another story. Although there is no more open bin space in main cabin, there is some space in the first-class bins. I ask permission of a first-class passenger if I may move his bag to the left so I can accommodate the man. He demands to know why. I explain why. He twists his arms into a pretzel on his chest and snorts at me, "Well ok, then." I give him a cold look and say, "Never mind, I can see that it's not ok." I go on to make an adjustment elsewhere with a more genial passenger. Let's be clear, here. I don't need his permission to move his bag. I considered it a simple courtesy to have first presented the issue to him. Generally speaking, flight attendant courtesies are rarely acknowledged and hardly ever thanked. Yet, I never had a passenger act so rankled about moving a bag twelve inches. It was *his* space, goddammit, even if it was empty space.

Lav Door Lock

The door to the lavatory on the A320 has a little metal flap. On the flap it says "LAVATORY." If you lift the flap, you will see a mechanism that will allow the flight attendant to release the locking bolt on the inside of the lav. This is not generally known by the public, and it is used only in the rare case of an emergency. In twenty-two years, I never lifted the flap for an emergency. But, if you open the flap and press your eye close to it, a passenger might mistakenly think you are actually looking into the lav itself.

We are on a flight from DC to Minneapolis. Al Franken, a Minnesota senator and former comedian, is onboard. Someone is already in the lav when Al comes back to use it. While he is standing there waiting his turn, I open the little flap, pretend to be looking into it, and say to Al, "It looks like she's about done, won't be long now." He laughs. I think he gets it. It seems as though a couple of people in line behind Al, however, are not so amused. I have to explain that I cannot see into the lav. But, I am quite pleased with myself. I got a humorist to laugh.

Buster

A woman gets on the plane and in big, capital letters across the front of her T-shirt, it says, "BUSTER." I can't help but notice that the shirt is perilously distorted and dangerously stressed by the size of the underlying topography. Male passengers, who with bored expressions have been staring blankly out their first-class windows, now swivel involuntarily in their seats as if their heads are magnetized by some irresistible Buster-beam. There is a certain tension in the air, which is broken when I ask the young man following the woman, "Are you Buster?" He smiles and says, "I could be." The woman may not even have been aware of any of this. But, as I said, I couldn't help but notice. I might have sprained an eyeball.

Mount St. Helen's

Another pneumatic woman gets on the plane with a T-shirt that displays a map of the state of Washington. I ask her if she can point out Mount St. Helen's. You can finish this one on your own.

Needle and Thread

A woman on the plane wonders if there is any needle and thread on the aircraft. She needs it for a few moments, not for any sewing, but to show the passenger sitting next to her some sort of trick. There is no needle and thread on the aircraft, but I have in my personal items a safety pin and some rubber bands. I dig this stuff out of my tote and loan it to her on her promise that she'll return it. She is sitting next to a woman who is pregnant, and she's going to use the rubber bands and safety pin to perform some sort of a trick to determine the sex of the baby. Later on, I happen to be in the aisle, and she hands me back my things. The rubber bands are now all joined together so tightly I can't get them apart. The safety pin is bent. No big deal. Rubber bands and safety pins are cheap. Those were my items, though, that I loaned to her, which she just took for granted. Why wouldn't an Airbus 320 on its way to Salt Lake City have needle and thread? No, "Thank you," just, "Here's your stuff." I guess the baby is going to be a boy. But, if the ritual requires needle and thread, and you use safety pins and rubber bands, I wonder what she's gonna get. I'm thinking: quality control agent in a rubber factory?

An Annual Recurrent Training (A.R.T.) Experience

(This is the boring exception I mentioned in the introduction. So, if you want to take a break, go out into the lobby for a cigarette—now is the time.)

There is a door at the back of the DC-9 aircraft that leads into the tail cone. It is opened by a handle in the center of the door at about eye level. Covering the handle is a plastic shield. Flight attendants will not open this door except in an emergency. The plastic shield is meant to remind the flight attendant not to touch the door handle. Sort of like a "break glass" admonishment covering a fire extinguisher housing. The flight attendant's jump seat is mounted on the front of this door. It will snap up flush against the door when it is not in use. If it didn't, the door to the tail cone wouldn't open fully. It is a very narrow space back there. Yet, two flight attendants can squeeze together to sit on this jump seat. To the left and right (just in front of the jump seat, facing forward) are the restrooms. When the door to the tail cone is open, it locks against the wall and blocks the door to the restroom. If someone were in the restroom, it would be impossible to get out. A normal flow of events in an emergency would ensure that that would not happen. What follows now are the steps involved in conducting an evacuation on the DC-9. Take notes, you may be tested on this. This is a reenactment of the A.R.T. test. In a real emergency, much will happen before we get to the part where the test begins, which is now.

I am sitting on the jump seat in the brace position, bent over forward and sitting on my hands. I hear the pilot over the P.A. say, "Evacuate the aircraft." He may say this three times. I need to hear it once. I start shouting, "Release your seatbelts, release your seatbelts." I release my seatbelt, too. Then I attach a barrier strap from one side of the aisle to the other. It is meant to keep passengers from crowding too close to the tail cone door, which opens inward. (If I forget to attach the strap, I can fail the test.) Now, I remove the plastic cover and open the tail cone door. I continue to shout, "Stay back, stay back!" When the door is open and locked against the wall, I release the barrier strap and remove the flashlight from its charging housing. (If I forget to detach the strap or grab the flashlight, I can fail the test.) I continue shouting, "Stay back, stay back!" even though I have removed the barrier strap, because the open door is not an exit from the aircraft. It is an entrance to the tail cone. It is a narrow, low space in there, and as I navigate the catwalk crouching low, I use the flashlight to look for the handle that will drop the tail cone. If the engines have not yet shut down, I prepare myself mentally for noise so loud and piercing, it could actually be disorienting enough to distract me from my task. I continue to shout, "Stay back, stay back!" There is still no clear exit from the aircraft. But, at least, it's dark. Pulling on this aforementioned handle will release the back part of the tail cone. I must pull with one hand, because I have a flashlight in the other. The aft section of the tail cone plummets to the ground. Now I can see outside, and I must assess conditions. If I see fire, I start shouting, "Go back, go back, exit blocked!" If the outside area is free and clear, I will deploy the slide. I am still shouting, "Stay back!" The slide pack is on the floor near my feet. I push it out and pull the strap that will cause the slide to inflate. If it inflates and is well positioned, the exit finally becomes useful. I stand off to the side on a little platform and start shouting (dry-throated and hoarse), "Come this way, stay low, sit and slide, help at the bottom, and take me with you!" The flashlight can help direct the passengers toward me if it is dark or smoky.

If I had survived a real evacuation, such as one like this, maybe I could have kept the flashlight as a souvenir of one of the most horrifying experiences of my life. A final note: It is my understanding that no major American airline has any DC-9 aircraft in service any longer.

Bambi Laughs

Don't get your hopes up. This ain't *Ninotchka*. Bambi is a lousy flight attendant. She isn't focused. She doesn't pay attention. She can't wait to sit down and read a magazine. She is almost entirely uncommunicative. She doesn't listen or hear when you say something to her, and then she will just talk over you when you are trying to point out something. Later in the trip, Bambi warms up to cool, even if she is wishing I didn't exist. She even laughs pretty vigorously once. Someone had left a book on the plane, *The Woman Next Door*. The cleaners had put the book in the magazine rack. I happen to come upon it, and I ask Bambi if she is interested in it. She says she had already noticed it and it didn't seem very interesting to her. I say, "Well, maybe if it had been titled *The Bitch Next Door*, it might have seemed more interesting." For some reason, in spite of the fact that my comment blows beneath her sarcasm radar, this just releases up her sense of funny. She laughs and laughs. Then she reads the back book cover to see what it is all about and figures somewhere in there that I am probably right with my invented title. That makes her laugh all over again. Me too, but for different reasons.

Newark Layover

In Newark, you go down to the bar for a beer. A little later, the first officer comes down, and even though you are pretty much finished with your drink and drained of will, you hang around—as much from inertia as anything else—to keep him company. These are dreamy, forgettable moments. The day has been long, the layover is short, the conversation dull. It takes an effort to recall where you were when you started your day, what day it is, even where you are now. The sharp circle of your sense of self gets fuzzy at the edges. You are with people you don't know. You're in a place you've never been before. It's late, and the lobby all around you is dark. The bar hovers in a halo of light disconnected from the rest of the real world. Real world? There's no one here to confirm that you are you. And you are . . . an exhausted creature with ebbing self-awareness, drinking. You and beer. The bartender is fairly inattentive. She needs to be summoned. She is busy with some strident regulars who are organizing their go-home. They are too drunk to drive. They need a cab but are too drunk to know it, so they argue. There's a young woman hanging out at the bar, and she is spouting profanities at a disturbingly shrill volume with no self-restraint. The captain has now arrived for a drink, and he is completely ignored by the bartender. She's preoccupied, like a mother hen, gathering up all of her chicks into safety, even though her chicks are drunk, obnoxious, and spouting profanities. The shrill, profane "chick" seems to be the blue ribbon of the night, and a couple of the young male rams nearly lock horns over her. Now the pilots are together, so they can ignore you. They were boring, anyway. They'll talk about vectors and wind sheers, and then they'll bitch about the company and their 401K. You remember that you are "just" a flight attendant. You don't need to babysit anymore, so you lumber off to your room, gravity sucking at your leaden legs. Maybe the next pilots will be higher on the evolutionary scale and will be able to communicate in sounds more sophisticated than grunts.

You are in your room now. You had been saving your personal stash of vodka for tomorrow's long layover, but, what the hell . . .

Nicky, Nicole

Nicky, I am told, looks a little like Nicole Kidman. That is, I suppose, if you take Nicole Kidman and make her about 5'4". Then if you give Nicole Kidman glasses, make her hair brown, wrap it up in a wad on top of her head. And then if you could make Nicole Kidman suck on something sour, then yeah, Nicky does look a little like Nicole. Oh, I forgot, you have to give Nicole a sex-change, too.

All On One Trip

A passenger is traveling alone with his own personal onboard wheelchair. Even so, we need to use the aircraft's aisle chair to get him to the lav. In order to do it we suspend the service, secure our beverage carts, release the aisle chair from its housing, get him in the aisle chair, secure his safety straps, help him into the lav, wait for him to finish his business, help him out of the lav, muscle him back into the aisle chair, secure his safety straps, return to his seat, get him back into it, return the aisle chair to its housing, and then continue our service.

A passenger is sick. He vomits with such generosity into the lav sink that it plugs up, and we have to close the lav for the rest of the flight.

A passenger is listed as "adult unaccompanied." Mr. Ricci doesn't seem to want to go with us and is wandering around the plane, trying to get off, insisting he's not going with us. Eventually, his people come on the plane and stay with him until the plane leaves. We are told he will ask to go to the bathroom, but since he has a Foley catheter, he won't need to urinate. Great.

A passenger riding in first class is so big that she dislodges an armrest. When offered peanuts from a basket, she fists up all of them, saying, *"I'm hongree!"*

A passenger takes off his shirt and cleans the mirrors in the lav. He comes out of the lav topless and says, "I did some work for you."

When this large passenger goes so completely and comfortably to sleep, he is unaware that his head now droops out over the aisle, and we have to step carefully when we pass him so we don't bang him or wake him. His shirt has crept up, and his pink belly rolls out like some over-inflated hot air balloon. He looks overdue.

Poor Kathleen. She is laughing so hard her eyes are leaking.

What, No Pepsi™?!

A passenger in the last row is complaining because we have run out of Pepsi. He is so self-righteous and indignant, not to mention rude, that both Beverly and Kathy have refused to serve him. He said we ought to have enough Pepsis for everyone on board. "How is Northwest going to compensate *me?*" was his laughable demand. Going a bit on his behalf beyond the line of tolerance, I offer him as much of anything else as he'd like. He is, of course, angling for free booze. He finally settles on orange juice, which, on the aircraft is made from a cheap concentrate and aircraft water. I plunk a whole full jug down in front of him. Unfazed, "That's good, 'cause I'm really thirsty." I'm glad I wasn't expecting a thanks, so I am happy, in a convoluted way, to have had my expectations met.

Now, there's a woman sitting just in front of Mr. Thirsty who asks me for a pillow. It takes me a while to find one, and when I hand it to her, I say, "This is the last pillow on the plane."

Mrs. Thirsty now pipes up and asks me for a pillow. She had to have heard what I just said. They were just bent on being nasty. I wonder how you compensate *her* for no pillow... I find her a blanket and tell her to roll it up into a pillow. (I should have told her that I inspected the blanket for those little, white squiggly things but didn't find any.) Today is not the day they are going to get something for nothing from the airline.

Polaroids, Milwaukee – Orlando

A guy asks me if we have a Bible on board. A Bible? "Don't you think you ought to have one? I bet the Gideons would be happy to put them on the planes." "Did you say 'giddy ones'?" Here's what I think: I can think of reasons why one might want to have a Bible on the plane, but then I think you should bring your own. And no, you can't borrow mine.

We're having a little bit of turbulence, and a woman asks me if it's normal for this flight. "Turbulence is normal, but not for any particular flight." Here is what I didn't say: "We were lucky today, the turbulence on this flight usually rips us out of our seats. Makes you feel like popcorn."

A guy wants some alcohol. So do I. He doesn't mean a drink—he means alcohol of the rubbing variety. I get him a couple of antiseptic wipes. He seems happy with that. I tell him not to drink them.

We're picking up trash after the service. As I approach her row, a woman at the window stands up, holding her trash in her hand. Her neck is bent, and her head is curled over on account of the overhead bins. "I have garbage, I have garbage!" she shouts out to me. She seems so pleased, as if she were holding up the winning bingo card. "Don't we all, don't we all," I say.

On arrival, a woman has a crying baby. While she fusses with her bags, another passenger holds the baby, which promptly stops crying. Pretty soon, Marci, one of the flight attendants, is holding the baby. At the aircraft door, the woman is obligated to take her baby back, which immediately starts crying. That makes Marci cry. She is worried about the baby.

All of the above in one day.

Pot Licker

We are delayed out of Minneapolis to Grand Rapids because of a frozen waste disposal line. Or, delayed on account of a toilet. There's a man in first class who already has had two drinks: screwdrivers. He flies this flight every week and, according to him, it's delayed every week for some reason. He thinks the aircraft is a piece of crap, and if the company would just buy American, this sort of thing wouldn't happen. He wants me to go and tell the pilots that the aircraft is a piece of crap and that they should tell the people in charge to buy American. I do this. I suppose I've had less reasonable passenger requests. Now, the pilot is on his second flight as an A320 captain. In the right seat is the instructor for his initial operating experiences, his IOE. I say, "There's a passenger in first class who wants me to tell you that this aircraft is a piece of crap and that you should tell your superiors to buy American." The pilots just don't have the receptors to be able to process what I've just said. Blank look. I go back and tell Mr. Screwdriver that I did what he asked me to do. Pretty soon, he himself gets up and goes to the cockpit to share with the pilots his insights. He knows everything. He's an engineer and a mechanic and a pilot, or so he claims. He knows it all and can't believe we're being held up by a toilet. Seen from that angle, he does have a point. But that bit about buying American identifies him as somebody who's been living off-planet for a time. Maybe he had an out-of-body experience and couldn't get back. Now he challenges me about not caring. "Look at you, you don't care." That's too personal an insult. I'm ready for a "coaching" for what I'm about to say next. I immediately stop everything I'm doing. I give him a look so cold that it freezes his eyes to mine, and I say, "You are wrong. I care about my job. I care about my image. I care about my passengers, and I care about the window I am, through which people see my company. And I did what you asked me to do." Surprisingly, he is smitten and now seems a little smaller in his seat. We arrive eighteen minutes late. It never comes back to me.

Next week comes along, and just by the mechanisms of scheduling I'm on the same trip. Prior to boarding, we find out two things. One is that we are going to be delayed, and two is that there is an incorrigible passenger waiting in the boarding area. I immediately know who it is. It's our "buy American" passenger from last week. As he steps on the plane, I shove a screwdriver in his hand. He says, "You pot licker." He's grinning, though. Getting off the plane in Grand Rapids, he wants to shake my hand. Whatever. I'm the guy that doesn't care.

Little Richard

Yes, *that* Little Richard. From about twelve or so, I have been a fan of Little Richard. Big fan! As a member of the Little Richard Fan Club, I received a beautiful, signed, 8x10, black and white glossy of him.

Imagine my delight when I meet him on a flight. He sits in first class at 3B on the aisle on the A320. He is kind and friendly. I tell him I have been a fan for nearly fifty years and he smiles, shakes my hand, and signs a bunch of stuff for me. That's all. No dirt, no secrets, just a starstruck old man meeting one of the icons of his youth. Actually, the icon was now pretty old, too.

Fur Coat

We are early in the boarding process, and the bins are still mostly empty. A man is set to throw his roller bag up into the overhead when I notice that a woman has laid out her fur coat on the full length of the floor of the bin. The man does not see the coat and it will certainly be soiled, if not damaged, if I don't rescue it. I do not know whose coat it is. That can be sorted out later. My plan is to save the coat, take it to the front, and hang it in the first-class cloak bustle. As I'm doing this, I hear behind me a sharp, annoyed voice shouting, "*What* are you doing with my coat?" The reverie of my intentions, of my actions, is completely shattered. My brain stumbles around for words. "Uh, I'm going to hang this in first class." She sniffs something at me in a venomous tone that I don't quite hear. It is a struggle to get up to first class, on account of the steady stream of boarding passengers. I brief the lead flight attendant. I can explain everything to the woman later. Of course, I understand what a woman might think if she sees someone carrying off her precious fur coat. But if you are a bitchy old lady and you see a handsome young man (me, a veritable cross between Cary Grant and George Clooney) with your coat, wouldn't your tone be just a touch more solicitous? More curious, less accusatory? As I return to the main cabin, I see Andrew, the other flight attendant, standing above the fur-coat woman speaking with a raised voice, "But he was only trying to save your coat!" For the rest of the flight, I have no further communication, not even eye contact, with the woman who warms herself with a dead animal.

Bill, and How I Touched Him

When the president of the United States goes on an international trip, he will fly on Air Force One, accompanied by a second plane with the press. This second plane is a commercial plane, hired usually from one of the legacy airlines. In the nineties, this situation fell to Northwest Airlines for a series of three press trips. We, at the Chicago O'Hare flight attendant base, were invited to be the crew on these trips.

In 1994, we are in Normandy, celebrating the fiftieth anniversary of the WWII invasion. The planes have landed, and President Clinton has agreed to meet us. We are standing in a line on the tarmac—maybe fifty or so of us, two or three deep—waiting for him to come by. A couple of black-suited security men come by, and we all must make our hands visible. Now the president comes by, smiling, with his arms reached out. As far as I can tell, he does not shake any hands. He merely touches the visible outstretched hands of the group. I am not in front. Still, he looks right at me as he brushes my fingers and says, "How was your flight?" Before I can answer, he is already touching the next batch of extended fingers. In a flash, I just became one-degree separated from a huge array of world leaders, as well as other celebrities.

I am aware that Clinton is a controversial person. Some of you might even be thinking, *"Ugh, if Clinton were to touch me, I'd want to go home and take a bath."* I understand that. I feel the same way about Trump. So, touché! The best thing about all of this is that we flight attendants get a guided tour of Air Force One. I even sit in the captain's cockpit seat.

Lone Ranger

A woman takes a seat in the first row of main cabin. This particular seat is clearly visible from first class, because of the unusual aisle alignment on the McDonnell-Douglas DC9s. Likewise, she has a clear view into first class, because the bulkhead is in front of the passengers sitting next to her. She prepares for the flight by putting a mask over her eyes. I guess she's expecting to nap. The aircraft door has been closed, and Nancy is sitting at her jump seat, preparing to read her predeparture safety instructions. I say to her, "Nancy, lean over and look back into the cabin, and tell me if you see anybody that reminds you of the Lone Ranger." She, of course, immediately sees the woman with the mask and completely loses it. I had not expected such an intense response. She, literally, is unable to read the safety demo script. Over the PA, we can hear her start, stop, giggle... and try unsuccessfully to continue. I'm standing at the front of main cabin, right next to mask-lady, with my demo oxygen mask. I am red-faced with the effort of trying not to laugh. The passengers, for some reason, seem to enjoy it. Even the "Lone Ranger" woman is beaming from the radiance of this shared gleeful moment.

The really funny thing about all of this is that it wasn't really all that funny. We got caught up in a moment.

Decaf

A man in first class requests a cup of decaf. I roll my eyes and tell him it will take a few minutes. Sometime later in the flight, my face suddenly flushes with embarrassment because I have just remembered that I rolled my eyes at a passenger who made a reasonable request. I immediately go to him and apologize. This is what I say. "I want to apologize to you, because when you ordered decaf, I think I rolled my eyes. I will explain. This airplane has three coffee makers, one in the first-class galley and two in main cabin. Each coffee maker has an extra extendable hot plate. So, at the very most, at any given moment, six pots of coffee could be available. Alas, if it were only ever true. My coffee maker in first class is not working at all. The coffee makers in main cabin are both working, but neither of the extendable hot plates are functioning. So, we are basically down to two pots of hot coffee. To prepare for what most passengers will want at this time of the day, the main cabin flight attendants have brewed regular coffee. Coffee for first class, decaf or otherwise, has to be retrieved from the main cabin galley. When I went to main cabin for your decaf, I knew that none would have been brewed. That's why I knew it would take a few minutes. I hope you can see now why I rolled my eyes. It should not be that difficult to serve coffee to our first-class passengers. Coffee! I am happy to have you with us today. If it weren't for you, I wouldn't have a job. I shouldn't have rolled my eyes at all, but sometimes, little frustrations escape. Just please, understand I did not roll my eyes because of your request." My apology is well received.

Jane Wyman

There is a woman on the plane who looks just like Jane Wyman. When I first saw her, I did a double take. Famous people must get used to this "look." And, people who look like famous people must get the "look," too. Anyway, when I looked at the Jane Wyman look-alike, I could see that she saw that I had just given her the "look." I kept looking at her as I came nearer, she looking at me. Then I said, "Naw, if you were her, you'd be up in first class." She laughed, because without any other words, we both knew what it was all about.

Turbulence

Luckily, our meal service is complete. I am standing in the back galley of Boeing's 757 when it strikes. It starts as a sharp, unexpected jolt. Then it gets worse. The rough, abrupt shakings of the plane are hard to describe unless you have experienced them. Turbulence combines up-and-down with left-and-right motions into a sort of twisty corkscrew whirl. In this case, I can barely hold on. I could not hold on with just one hand. I would need both hands just to lower my jump seat and strap in. So, I work my way around to the last row of seats and sit on the lap of the nearest passenger and instruct him to hold onto me. For an eternity (maybe five, six minutes), he hugs me in nervous, wide-eyed safety. During these crazy moments, a man in the row in front of us turns and hands me some trash. I refuse it and tell him I will get it later.

I'll pause here for a moment while you process that.

After we descend to a "more comfortable cruising altitude," the pilot comes on the PA and explains that the turbulence was completely unexpected. It isn't an apology. When we land, at least one-third of the passengers are either crying or have thrown up. Or both.

Heineken™

Passengers may not consume their own alcohol on the plane. This is a good rule, especially if you imagine a wedding party on their way to Vegas with a dozen people drinking from their own vodkas. So, when a man, after settling in for the flight, opens a can of his own beer, I have to step in. I inform him of the regulations and that I must confiscate his beer. I think it was a Budweiser™. He is not happy, but he complies. He thinks that I should at least provide for him a complimentary beer, since I have just taken his away. I tell him that alcohol is an accountable item and that I can't do that. His response is, "You can do it, but you won't." That stings. And as my brain is building up defensive responses, I can feel them start to crumble. After a few minutes of clear thinking, I go back to him and say, "You are right. I *can* do this. We have Heineken™ and Miller Lite™. Would you prefer one over the other?" He seems pleased. Maybe even slightly upgraded, he chooses the Heineken™.

Movie

We are on our way from Chicago to Tokyo. Onboard, we will have time for maybe two movies. There are different movies for the Chicago-Tokyo flight than for the Tokyo-Chicago flight. This is so passengers going from one to the other will not get the same movie on the return. Now a man is not happy with his choices and would rather watch one that will be available on the Tokyo-Chicago return. I explain to him the situation and I, of course, can't just remove a movie from the player that is already in progress. He seems put out. I tell him that when the currently-running movie is over, I will slide one of his liking into the player for him, although it will be against the policy to play movies unscheduled for that particular flight. It will make hardly any difference. Everyone will be asleep anyway. To be sure, when I return to tell him that I am ready to insert his movie, he is, in fact, asleep. I will not wake him. I monitor his progress for a couple of hours. When he wakes up, I tell him that I can start up his movie, and... he waves me off. He waves me off! He does not win the medal for the rudest passenger ever—that's another story—but he does get a spot on the podium.

Let's review. I agree to do him a favor that conflicts with procedures. For hours, I monitor his situation so that I can complete his request. Then, when I am about to accomplish this favor, he interrupts me wordlessly by waving me off. I get a sense of what "chopped liver" must feel like.

We're Here to Save Your Ass, Not Kiss It

I know, it's not meant to be a literal statement. If a flight attendant should ever save your life, he or she would not leave your behind behind. We do not deliver assless passengers to safety. But kissing it? Well, yeah! That's what we do. Hour after hour, day after day, we serve people, we attend to their needs and accommodate their requests. Remember, it's not literal. In an entire career, one may never act in an emergency or ever use emergency equipment (like my career). We serve, but we are not sycophants. Period. We are mostly here to "kiss your ass" and only, in vanishingly rare situations, save it.

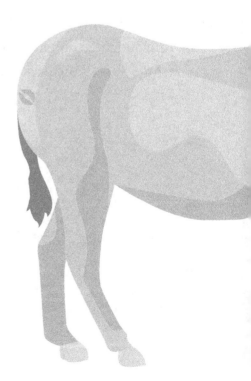

Cigarette

A guy on the plane is at door five, aircraft-left on the 747. We are on our way to Detroit, and he is calmly smoking. I tell him that he is in violation of FAA rules and must extinguish his cigarette. He says, challengingly, "And if I don't?" I say, "I will communicate to you an actual future: I will go to the captain, and I will tell him that we will need law enforcement to greet the plane. He will ask me why, and I will say that a passenger refuses to put out his cigarette. He will say, 'Ok.' When we get to Detroit, you will be first to get off the plane, escorted by Detroit's finest. You will march past all of the other passengers who are impatiently waiting to deplane. If anyone should ask me about it, I will say, 'He did not follow instructions.' The following details of your arraignment are unclear other than the great state of Michigan will be picking up the tab for your lodging tonight." He puts out his cigarette, and in that moment becomes the least interesting person on the plane.

Buffalo

The four of us—pilot, first officer, Emily, and I—are on our layover in a car, on our way to Niagara Falls. The pilot is driving the car. Emily and I are in the back seat. The best thing I can say about Emily is that her callipygian contours are more striking than the contents of her cranium. We are proceeding south, and we know that the Falls are off to our left, to the east. Emily sees a sign that says "Niagara Falls – Exit Right." At the bottom of the exit ramp, we know that we must turn left, to the east. But Emily is energetically maintaining that we must turn right, as the sign had said. The pilot, a kind soul, does not want to contradict her adamant certainty. I try to explain to Emily that we need to go east. *East, west* mean nothing to her. Finally, I say, "You can tell by the sun what direction we are going." Emily bellows, "What the hell does the sun have to do with it?" A thin smile creeps onto the pilot's face. We turn left (east) and have a nice day at the Falls.

Rag Doll

We are getting on a flight continuing to Denver and are informed that we need to protect a seat cover because a woman "lost control" and there hasn't been time to clean up. So, during the frantic time between flights, we gather up a couple of blankets, some plastic, and prepare a dry place for her to sit. The woman who lost control and is continuing with us to Denver is, figuratively, a bag of bones, a rag doll, arms askew and angled off in improbable directions. Probably from birth, she has had severe developmental disabilities. Even though, that doesn't quite convey the image. The woman who would have sat next to her wants no part in this drama and wanders off to find another seat, since we are far from being full. The woman who is in such need is accompanied by a caregiver who can pick her up, put her down, put her in her seat or wheelchair, as if she were a small house pet. To my estimation, she has no awareness at all. I greet her, but there is no response. I'm not sure if she is able to move her head and look in my direction, much less focus. The caregiver, maybe a daughter, maybe a professional, is on the fast track toward sainthood. What on Earth keeps them going? Symbiosis?

In the meantime, I hope the Cubbies won today. That means I hope the Giants lost. And then wouldn't it be nice if everything (everywhere for everybody) was just . . . nice.

118

Milk

Ann and I are working a beverage service in the main cabin. I am still a fairly junior flight attendant. Ann is senior to me by fifteen years. She starts her beverage cart from the back of the plane, near the galley, and works forward. I pull my cart to the front, right at the first-class curtain, and work aft. Conducting the service in this manner is frowned upon by management, who would prefer that we both start at the front and work back together, bumping up as we go along. What we are doing has certain concrete advantages. For one, passengers in the last row, for a change, will get served first. Also, the flight attendant working forward will have easy access to the aft galley if anything else is needed. Near the beginning of my service, a passenger requests milk. Although milk has been catered in the galley, I have none on my cart. Ann can bring me some milk from the galley if I can get her attention. I ring the passenger's call button, and Ann looks up. I have trouble communicating to Ann, without yelling, what I need. Then I remember that I have a latex glove in my apron pocket. We wear these gloves when we pick up the meal service trays. I get out the glove and blow into it until all of the fingers are full and taut. When I hold the glove up with the fingers pointing down, it looks like udders. I grab a latex finger, squeeze, and pull. Now Ann knows what I need, as do about one hundred passengers. Ann gets the milk, comes storming out of the galley, nearly upsets her cart trying to get around it, stomps up the aisle, throws the milk onto my cart, and bursts, "I have never seen anything like that before!" And then she completely loses it. She is literally doubled over with laughter, as are a number of passengers who have been watching this comedy. Ah, showbiz!

Religion

It's a light load and a bright, shiny day. The last few rows are empty. I take a center seat in the last row, aircraft right, and prepare to eat my crew meal. A passenger ambles back and glues himself to the seat in front, facing me. He folds his arms over the back of the seat and says, "Takin' a little break?"

"Yeah," I go.

"How do you like your job?"

"Well, I've been doing it for about twenty years now, so, uh, I guess it's ok. The food pellets are good."

Already I'm not liking this. I notice he has a Bible tucked under his arm. I'm thinking I should have hidden in the galley and taken my lunch standing up, but hey, it's a light load and a bright, shiny day. Why not be comfy?

"I'll bet you spend a lot of nights in hotels."

I take that as a question and, "About a hundred a year," I answer. I'm not being very glib.

"Have you ever had any close calls?"

"No, not really, or none that I was ever aware of. I've had my share of aborted landings and takeoffs, had some pretty rough turbulence, been struck by lightning—but nothing that could be considered a close call."

"What would you do if you were going to crash?"

"I'd do my best to prepare the passengers and the cabin according to well-rehearsed instructions."

"How would you prepare yourself?"

"After I had prepared the cabin and passengers, I'd go to my jump seat, assume the position, review my commands, and await instructions from the pilot. But that isn't what you meant, is it?"

"Not really. Are you prepared to die?"

"No, of course not, but if you're wondering if I read the Gideon Bible when I spend all those nights in hotels, the answer is no. I've read enough Bible in my life, and I got the message."

"Do you consider yourself a Christian?"

"I've got no problem with Christ. I sometimes have a problem with Christians."

"What do you mean?"

"I mean people who pound their chest and broadcast their Christianity, but behave as though they've just stepped out of the cave and are ready to club or kill the first thing that comes along, even if it's another human being, a fellow human who doesn't have the right skin color or ethnic purity or other ideological or genetic or sexual orientations that are unfamiliar or unsavory to the 'card-carrying' Christian."

"Uh..."

"I'll just say this: Christ was inclusive! He gathered to himself the lowlifes of his social world: the tax collectors, women, even the dead! He elevated a Samaritan—*a Samaritan!*—and challenged us all to be like the Samaritan. So, I don't have a problem with Christ or Christians or Christianity."

In the meantime, my meal is settling into a sort of brown, cold sludge, and the dessert is more and more resembling a puddle.

"Ok, fair enough. So, what do you think will happen to you after you die?"

"How would I know that?"

"God has a promise for you that Christ articulated in his message in the Bible."

"So, then, are you saying that you know what will happen to you after you die?"

"I hope to be united with God and spend eternity in paradise."

"I hope for your sake that you are right. It's a matter of faith, though, isn't it? I just don't enjoy your confident certainty."

"But, it's all in the Bible!"

"It's not all in the Bible. There are no airplanes in the Bible, or microwaves, or cell phones, assault weapons, there are not even any rotary telephones or hand calculators or toasters in the Bible. A lot is in the Bible, but not all. But I'm guessing you believe in the literal message of the Bible?"

"Of course!"

"Like the story of Adam and Eve, Noah's ark, Jonah and the whale, Daniel and the lions, Mary and the virgin birth, Christ reviving the dead Lazarus, turning water into wine, and returning to life after being crucified to walk to Emmaus and showing his death wounds to Thomas?"

"Sure."

"You know, there's over 50,000 species of just mollusks. So, I'm thinking how tough that's gotta be for Noah, with 100,000 of nothing but mollusk. And amphibians, insects, mammals. Really big ark, I guess."

"Well, I believe that with God, all things are possible."

"I prefer to believe that with God, all things are reasonable."

"God works in mysterious ways."

"That's a dodge, and you know it! And it makes me crazy! So, when a tsunami kills 100,000 people, you say, 'It's God's will!' Or when Tebow connects on a spectacular pass, wow, he is favored by God, but when he's intercepted or sacked, the 'mysterious ways' folks are mysteriously silent. Do you really think God has favorites in the NFL?"

"Like I said, God works in mysterious ways."

"I suppose I can't argue that point. So, God doesn't have to work in reasonable ways. He can make the sun stop, He can reverse gravity, and He can crowd 100,000 mollusks on the ark. You know, just for the sake of truth, even God cannot make pi equal to 3."

"He can if He wants to. We just cannot know the ways and designs of God."

"Well, that, my fellow traveler, is where we part ways. We *can* know the designs of God, it's just that He does not reveal them to us all at once. That's why we of our age walked on the moon and not the ancient Greeks. Maybe it is still the sixth day, and God hasn't rested yet. Or, maybe it's still only the first day."

Sardines

Tom and I are visiting with a rubber-faced old gentleman who wanted to tell us some of his war stories. Tom was telling us about a time when a passenger had brought a cheap can of sardines on the plane, and when opened, it really stank. This reminded the old fella about a time when the US army was taking over Düsseldorf and how clever the Germans had been at hiding their booty. Well, he and his buddies discovered an artificial wall in a captured German's basement. They had noticed it because the above ground floor plan didn't match the basement size. So, they broke through this fake wall and found the German's stash of wine, champagne, beer and . . . Portuguese sardines! He tells us about it like these Portuguese sardines were the creme de la creme or something. So they feasted on beer and sardines. The guy says that he ate probably about four cans of sardines . . . and has never again eaten another one! He tells us he was burping sardine for six months. I imagine this old man to be a widower and think that maybe he doesn't have many people to talk to. He seems to get such a pleasure out of telling his story. If he can be reminded of a story just because somebody says "sardine," I wonder how many other random words will trigger other wonderful stories.

Screaming Babies

I think the babies on the plane have a code. One baby screams and screams. It's screaming that it's hungry. Another baby thinks, *"Hey, I'm hungry, too,"* and screams. Pretty soon, all the babies on the plane are hungry and screaming. Then it's quiet for a little while. Then, all of a sudden, there's a shrill scream, "Are we there yet?" Another baby thinks, *"Yeah, man, are we there yet?"* Scream, scream, scream. Now the drug wears off the dog in the under-seat kennel, and it hears the screams. The screams hurt the dog's ears, and it starts to howl. Howl. Howl. Now a wrinkled, old passenger of indeterminate gender hears the dog howl and starts pounding on the call button and wailing, "Is there a dog around here? I'm allergic to dogs." Then a baby thinks, *"Hey, I'm allergic to dogs, too."* Scream. Howl. Scream.

Reality Check

I'm in Atlanta now, alone, on a single pattern. It's a long lay-over, so I'll be taken downtown in a limo. As we are leaving the airport, I see the driver look out of the window at a woman who is bending over and putting something into the trunk of a van. He is honking and waving. She turns and waves back. I wave, too. The driver is smiling broadly. He says to me, "She goes to our church. She's mighty fine. I try to do the right thing, though." I say, "Praise Jesus." He laughs and says, "That's for sure." The mood in the limo is breezy. His cell phone rings. It gets real quiet in the van. All I hear him say is, "Yes, dear."

Standing Room Only

We're on our way to Dallas. A tall, rugged man has gotten on, looking like a cowboy, or maybe the Marlboro Man. He says he needs to stand a bit. Turns out, he really does need to stand a bit. Earlier, when he landed in Bemidji, his plumbing had stopped working, and he had to go to the emergency ward. Well, they drained him, and six hours later, he was back in the emergency ward. This time, they inserted a catheter, so now he is on his way home, with a catheter. He says they told him that his prostate was enlarged, which was "normal" for men of his age. Now, he's headed home to see his urologist. Maybe a bit too much information, but hey, we are good to him and let him stand as much as he wants. It must be doubly uncomfortable with his height *and* a catheter, to sit all folded up in the seat. There's a woman on the plane who could very well be the biggest woman I've ever seen on an airplane. She needs two seat belt extenders, and she makes up for height in width. She needs to stand a bit, too—not only for herself, I presume, but to make it a bit more comfortable for the passengers sitting next to her. Well, with her and the "cowboy" both up and about, all the standing room is taken. We could hang a sign, "Seating room only." I am thinking that I want to get a picture of the two of them, if for no other reason than to prove that flight attendants do allow passengers to stand on occasion.

Chicago Tribune

Renee can't believe that a passenger has thrown the entire *Chicago Tribune* on the floor and just lets it lie there in the middle of the aisle. Getting into her good flight attendant mode, she goes to gather up all the sections. As she's picking up the loose pages, vomit drools out and gets all over her arms. She's nearly traumatized with disgust. Then she notices a woman lying on the floor, the likely perpetrator. Thomas says, "Maybe she read something that didn't agree with her."

Tide and Skepticism

A woman gets on this flight carrying a large box of Tide! I tell her I want to see that all her clothes are clean by the time we got to Detroit. Also, a guy gets on the plane with a T-shirt that says, "Skepticism is a virtue." I tell him I'm not sure I believe that. He doesn't get it.

Tomato Juice

This flight attendant keeps trying to fix me. I don't need fixing. She challenges me for drinking tomato juice. "Tomato juice is the worst thing you can drink," she scolds. That's not true. Battery acid is worse. Manure shakes, palmetto roach juice, mercury, liquid lead, paint thinner, anything laced with anthrax, blender spun weasel . . .

Louis

"CHICKEN OR BEEF?" is what the flight attendant over on the other aisle is shouting at the now-smitten Japanese man. It has never failed to astonish me that grown human beings can come to understand a foreign language if it is just spoken loudly enough. Sure. We are serving dinner on the long flight from Tokyo to Chicago. The meals are wrapped in foil. Some of the foil is plain, some has red stripes on it. This is how we tell which is chicken, which is beef. I am serving beverages behind Lou, who is serving the meals. Lou is a young man, senior to me only by two weeks. Both of us have been flying for less than a year. Then I see Lou do something that literally changes my life as a flight attendant. He is serving some folks who do not speak English. He holds one of the meals in front of the passenger and pulls back the foil so the passenger can see the contents. Then he does the same with the other choice. The passenger smiles, selects, and we move on. Wow! How much better is that than shouting? Or, in my case, clucking or mooing. I am so moved by the kindness and patience Lou demonstrates that I take it as a lesson for the rest of my career. He is the flight attendant I want to be. Having said that, Lou is not the exception. Lou is the general rule. Please keep that in mind, as I have reported on other rare, less accommodating examples in these pages.

Two Rudest Guys

They look like a blonde surfer dude and an older salt-and-pepper sugar daddy. They sit in the last row of first class, 3A and 3B. And, by God, they are going to try everything that first class has to offer. For starters, I open all the different types of wine, because they want to try them all. During the service, one of them wants red wine and sparkling water with a lime. The other one wants white wine and regular water with a lemon. Each time one of them rings the call button, the other one wants something, too. Over and over, I am called to their row to fill their water, refill their wine. They ring their call button so often that the other passengers are looking at me and wondering if I am going to explode. It is not without a little sarcasm that, after I'm finishing the service and am about to go back to help in the main cabin, I say to the two rudest guys ever, "I am going to help the other flight attendants. If you need anything, just ring your call button." As if I needed to say that. I have not been gone for more than a minute when these guys ring me. With exaggerated politeness, I ask them what it is I can do for them. This is their response: "Oh, we don't need anything. We just didn't think you would come." They seem to be at least as pleased with the flight as they are with themselves, because as they deplane, they give me a business card and tell me to call when I am in Pittsburgh, because they throw great parties. As their card, in one smooth uninterrupted motion, sails into the trash bin, I'm thinking, *"Sorry, can't make it. Busy. Gotta go to the store."*

Unaccompanied Adult

We are taking care of an elderly woman who is traveling as an "unaccompanied adult." She is on her way to Reno to visit her sister. Her daughter brought her on the plane and got her settled in. The daughter told the mother to, "Stay right there." And the mother does. She does not budge. Rip van Winkle moved more in his sleep than mother does on the flight from Saginaw to Minneapolis. In Minneapolis, we have trouble getting her off the plane for her connecting flight to Reno. She doesn't understand the concept of a connecting flight. She is expecting to be greeted now by her sister. She is determined to, "Stay right there." Minneapolis ground personnel are now responsible for her future. She is so tiny, though, and she responds so sweetly when I ask her if she would like something to drink. "Peps . . ." she says. Just Peps—a metaphor for another story we won't see the end of.

Worst Room Ever

We are riding in the van to our layover in Newark. We get to talking about our worst hotel experiences. The usual: bad service, bad food, bad beds, temperature, bugs, noise. The first officer has the best story. His walls were so thin! How thin were they? They were so thin that when he sneezed, the guy in the next room over said, "Gesundheit." True story.

Wright Brothers

While on duty, I am required to display a photo ID. I am also to carry with me my passport. In my wallet is my driver's license. So, for every moment of my career, while on duty, I have carried three forms of photo ID. As if that isn't enough, at some point, I was "certified." That means, I am "really" a flight attendant, even though I have already been flying for years. The certification card has an image of the Wright Brothers on it. The card has no official significance. I keep my certification card in a separate little black leather case. One day, as I am preparing for my flight and organizing my belongings for departure, I lose track of my little black wallet. At just about the time when I realize that it is missing, I hear an announcement, "Will Philip Bauer please report to gate 34." I know immediately why I am being paged. Someone found my wallet. I approach the gate, and the agent looks at me questioningly, holds up the card so she can see me and the image of the Wright Brothers on the card, and says, "You don't look anything like your picture." It would be funny if she weren't being serious. Maybe she thinks I am an imposter—or even worse, a terrorist. Maybe she's never heard of the Wright Brothers. I show her my ID badge and my passport. She is not convinced. Finally, another agent comes over, takes a look at me and the certification card, and bursts out laughing. She hands my card back to me and then snatches it right back. She needs to show this to some of her colleagues before I can get it back. For another round of laughs.

Don't Look Out the Window

We have a light load coming into Raleigh-Durham. Sometimes, I like to sit in the last row and look out the window. I tell Christina that I'll come to my jump seat when the landing gear goes down. I'm looking out the window, and I see another aircraft in the distance. As I'm watching, it looks like it's coming toward us. I know that at night, things can be deceiving. But still, it keeps getting closer. We're on our final approach. All of a sudden, we start to climb pretty sharply, even though our gear goes down. After we climb a bit, the gear goes back in, and the pilot comes on the PA and says that we have to go around again for sequencing. Later, when I talk to the pilots about it, they act like it was nothing out of the ordinary, although one of them says we were on a collision course, and it was bad air traffic control. I guess that will teach me to go looking out the windows, huh?

First Day Exhaustion

When you get up early on your first day and then fly until really late, it can set the tone for the rest of the trip. Vicky is minimally psychologically equipped for that sort of fatigue. Maybe it will get better. In the aisle she is nice, or at least ok with passengers, but in the galley it's "I wish that kid would just shut the fuck up." We are getting along fine, but her patience fuse is pretty short. Yesterday, she said to the last person, who is a little pokey getting off the plane, "Will it be today?" Let it go, girl.

Ring

In the lavatory—on a 747, on a flight from Singapore to Tokyo—I find a petite sterling silver ring. It features a kitten head, which stretches out into a long tail that forms the ring part. I have a passing impulse to put it in my pocket. But no. Instead, I am walking down the long 747 aisle, holding the ring aloft, and periodically announcing my find. "Did anyone lose this ring? I have found a ring in the lav. Is it yours?" A woman raises her hand, gains my attention, and tells me it must be hers. I tell her that secretly I was hoping no one would claim it, because I could have given it to my wife, who loves cats, and that I had a guilty impulse to just put it in my pocket. "And that is just what you should do," she says. "On, no," I say. "Forgive me, I wasn't angling." She replies, "Number one, you could have put it in your pocket, but you didn't. Number two, I got the ring in Jakarta, and when I go back, I can easily get another one." I say, "Are you sure?" She says, "I insist!" I express to her my sincere gratitude. Later, I find out that I was right. My wife, Sarah, loves the ring. In fact, she's wearing it today.

Palmetto

In Singapore, I purchase a little package of rubber palmetto bugs. A palmetto bug, essentially, is a big roach. Later, I am the lead flight attendant on the flight from Singapore back to Tokyo. The rest of the crew is an all-Asian mix of flight attendants who are based in any one of Northwest's South Asia destinations: Tokyo, Seoul, Hong Kong, Taipei, and of course, Singapore. The flight from Singapore to Tokyo

133

can take seven to eight hours. The crew is entitled to a crew meal. It is a full flight, so, as usual, the flight attendants will eat their meal standing up, in the galley, with their meal tray on the galley counter. There are three of us. To my right are two petite female flight attendants. Well into our meal, without them noticing, I pop one of the rubber bugs into my mouth. Then, they hear me exclaim with exaggerated disgust, "Ugh, what the . . . ?" They look in my direction and see me gag into my hand a mess of chewed food with the palmetto bug clearly visible. Brilliant. They might have screamed if they weren't afraid of waking first class passengers. Instead, they bounce up and down as if they are marching to an insanely rapid beat, hold up their arms, and clap their fists together as if they are furiously clanging some invisible cymbals. Once everyone has settled down and it is safe to laugh, one of them says, *"Oh, Mista Bowa, you so funny!"*

Hiccups

The last flight of my career is from Frankfurt, Germany to Detroit. It is on a DC-10. Toward the end of the flight, I hear an announcement congratulating me on my retirement. I am near the back of the plane, and nearly all of the passengers are clapping. This is the only time as a flight attendant that I have ever been applauded.

The only time? Well, one time long before, a woman summoned me to her seat. She seemed to be in some distress. It turned out that her little boy had the hiccups. It's flattering, in a way, the faith passengers bestow on flight attendants. I am not a magician, so I told her I didn't know how to cure hiccups. Yet, inexplicably, I said,

"But I can show him a magic trick." Most people know that magic involves more showbiz than manipulating the supernatural. So, I made a whole thing out of it. I said that I needed a quarter. Not a dime. Not a nickel. A quarter. I pressed the quarter with some fanfare into the little boy's hand and told him that I was going to make the quarter disappear—right out of his hand. I instructed him to hold it tightly in order to keep me from making it go away. I got a stern look of concentration on my face. I closed my eyes. I spread out all ten of my fingers and pointed them at his clenched fist, then I pronounced the magical incantation, "Fribbin on the ding-dang, globbin' on the clotch. And now if you open your hand, the quarter will have disappeared." Of course, the quarter was still there! For a moment, you could feel a wave of disappointment. But then I said, "But wait, the hiccups have disappeared!" And, indeed, they had. The few passengers who were watching all of this were delighted. They clapped. Some passengers away from the action turned and looked to see what the clapping was all about. I turned, too, and said to nobody, "Are you getting a picture of all of this?"

CPSIA information can be obtained
at www.ICGtesting.com
Printed in the USA
BVHW030846210922
647590BV00014B/294